1/18

STOPSPENDING
STARTMANAGING

STOPSPENDING

Strategies to Transform Wasteful Habits

STARTMANAGING

TANYA MENON •• LEIGH THOMPSON

Harvard Business Review Press

Boston, Massachusetts

Copyright 2016 Harvard Business School Publishing Corporation
All rights reserved
Printed in the United States of America

10 9 8 7 6 5 4 3 2 1

No part of this publication may be reproduced, stored in or introduced into a retrieval system, or transmitted, in any form, or by any means (electronic, mechanical, photocopying, recording, or otherwise), without the prior permission of the publisher. Requests for permission should be directed to permissions@hbsp.harvard.edu, or mailed to Permissions, Harvard Business School Publishing, 60 Harvard Way, Boston, Massachusetts 02163.

The web addresses referenced in this book were live and correct at the time of the book's publication but may be subject to change.

Cataloging-in-Publication data is forthcoming.

ISBN: 9781422143025
eIBSN: 9781625270559

The paper used in this publication meets the requirements of the American National Standard for Permanence of Paper for Publications and Documents in Libraries and Archives Z39.48-1992.

Contents

Acknowledgments   *vii*

CHAPTER 1

How Spending Substitutes for Managing   1

CHAPTER 2

The Expertise Trap   33

CHAPTER 3

The Winner's Trap   63

CHAPTER 4

The Agreement Trap   91

CHAPTER 5

The Communication Trap   119

CHAPTER 6

The Macromanagement Trap   147

CHAPTER 7

From Wicked Problems to Workable Solutions   177

Notes   *193*

Index   *211*

About the Authors   *219*

Acknowledgments

One of our job perks as faculty members is that we're surrounded by brilliant managers and executives who push our thinking every time we teach a class. Often this learning occurs after our classes, when we're shutting down our PowerPoints and packing up our laptops. That's when our students approach the podium and challenge us in unique ways.

Through these conversations, we've come to recognize three main types of questioners. One is hungry for even more ideas—they ask us for more books and more theories to deepen their understanding of the ideas. The second is primarily problem-focused. These executives are frustrated with a specific situation, and they often take over our blackboards, laying out their organizational structure, the personalities of the people involved, and all of the details of their all-consuming problem. They want results *now*.

This book is dedicated to a third type of executive in our classes—those who combine both of these approaches. They are interested in "ideas with legs" and want to take the knowledge and put it into action. They're often exceptionally humble—they're looking inward at themselves and they know they can do more with their knowledge, talents, and people. Along with introspection, these executives are also looking outward—taking ideas to their teams and experimenting with those ideas to push their own and others' potential. This book is the result of our decades of conversations with these unique individuals. They've shown us firsthand how executives facing apparently impossible problems find creative solutions and achieve action with traction.

This book builds on ideas from many fields, but particularly management and psychology. We'll highlight some of our own research findings in this area, which have been conducted in close collaboration with our advisers, our students, and other faculty members. We've jointly created, developed, and tested ideas with these colleagues, sometimes for over a decade, and they've profoundly influenced how we think and write. We're appreciative of support from our respective universities, the Fisher College of Business at the Ohio State University and Kellogg School of Management at Northwestern University. We're particularly indebted to the team at the Kellogg Team and Group Research Center (KTAG) who provided research support: Joel Erickson, Ellen Hampton, and Larissa Tripp, and the editorial help of Craig Boreth, Tessa Brown, and Zoe Mendelson. Our primary editor at Harvard Business Review Press, Courtney Cashman, and also Melinda Merino embody the insightful spirit of individuals who so naturally move between the world of ideas and pragmatic action. Finally, we would like to thank our invisible collaborators—our parents, husbands, and children—who never appear as our coauthors on papers or as our business associates, but who offer us wisdom and support no matter what.

CHAPTER 1

How Spending Substitutes for Managing

For the past year, Sandeep had been leading what he called "a team in name only."[1] At this point, he felt down for the count. He took a moment to consider how things had gotten so dysfunctional, and at what cost.

As a senior executive at a multinational software company, Sandeep was tasked with developing a strategic vision and getting buy-in from the high-level players on his cross-functional team. Facing new competitors in an already crowded market, he had little room for error. But even before he took over, the odds were against him. His two predecessors had spent upward of $5 million on surveys, focus groups, ethnographies, and market analyses. In the end, they failed to implement a functional strategic vision. One of the previous leaders had been demoted, and the other had left the company.

Now it was Sandeep's turn at the helm. He immediately discovered that the marketing and technical groups on this team were incapable of agreeing on which projects to pursue. The marketing group wanted to move product quickly and reduce offerings to only the most successful products. The technical group wanted to pursue several different projects at different stages of development. To the technical folks, the marketing focus was "small picture." To marketing, the tech group's ambitions were "pie in the sky" and impractical. Meetings were contentious, inefficient, and counterproductive.

Sandeep did his best to break the stalemate. To try to get the group talking, he created opportunities for regular video-conference updates. Yet the patterns of deadlock persisted. When he initiated one-on-one conversations with team members, all he got was finger-pointing. He spent thousands of dollars organizing an off-site retreat that was no more productive than the conference calls. Both groups continued to advocate their preferred solutions without listening or learning from each other.

Sandeep hired yet another consultant, who proposed yet another user ethnography. On this, at least, both tech and marketing sides agreed: "We want insight and action—not more research."

Finally, having gained no traction on any of his efforts, Sandeep knew he had no choice but to ask the two strongest (and most obdurate) personalities on either side to step down from the group so he could dismantle the coalitional dynamics. He had no illusions about how this strategy would be perceived by the overall group. "It will be terrible," he conceded.

We asked Sandeep to calculate how much this impasse had cost the company. As a highly analytic thinker, he took this question quite literally. Pulling out his calendar, he backtracked to when he first took over the team. His only real expense was the several thousand dollars he spent on the off-site and consultants, nowhere near the $5 million his predecessors had converted into beautifully bound reports and PowerPoint decks.

But then he examined a typical week, flagging all the relevant meetings, engagements, and presentations and noting how many people were involved in each "time sink," as he referred to the wasted energy and time. After a few moments of painful calculation itemizing the person-hours wasted in dysfunction, he said, "Hours are not even the right metric—we are talking *months* of squandered time!" When he included the missed business opportunities as well, Sandeep estimated that well over $5 million in lost time and productivity had evaporated.

Getting Traction on Your Hardest Problems

In our work as business school professors and consultants, we've met countless managers like Sandeep who, despite their sophisticated training and best intentions, fail to achieve their goals. They've come up against problems that refuse to budge no matter how hard they push. As gritty and persistent as managers are, at some point, they all face people problems that sap their time, money, and energy without producing results. Indeed, such problems may even get worse the harder they try to solve them. At first, managers may not see the signs of the money pit, but eventually the reality of investment without return becomes inescapable. And, perhaps, like Sandeep, you've said, "Enough is enough."

To investigate the price of what we call *action without traction*, we surveyed eighty-three senior executives (70 percent male; 87 percent with more than ten years of work experience, with 45 percent having ten years or more in senior management roles) from a range of different industries, countries, and functions.[2] We asked them to identify their most critical people problem at work and estimate the company's expenditures in dealing with just that one issue. On average, they estimated that the problem had cost them $15,470,289.99 and 5,514 hours and that, on average, 357 people in their organizations could have been doing something else other than dealing with the issue. We left this survey open-ended so executives could generate their own numbers. These were their perceptions, not scientific calculations, but they pointed to the magnitude of resources wasted on these issues.

We then asked the executives to identify, from a list of problem-solving approaches, all the things that their organizations were doing to try to solve the problem: 68 percent reported discussing the problem in meetings, 43 percent were conducting analyses, 36 percent had hired a consultant, 23 percent had fired people, 30 percent had hired more people, and 11 percent had taken other actions. Only 20 percent had done "basically nothing" to address the problem.[3] Executives estimated that there was a 46 percent chance that these approaches would solve the problem. In spite of all this spending, only 16 percent believed that it would be possible to purchase a solution; 60 percent believed that it was impossible to purchase the solution, and 24 percent were unsure whether such a solution could be bought.

In other words, managers are trying to solve intractable people problems in any way they can. They're exhaustively using all their skills to find solutions—spending time, energy, and money in the process—yet these problems still persist.

If you have ever experienced this feeling of action without traction in your own work, then this book is for you. We wrote it so that managers can stop spending and start managing. Most of the leaders and managers we have worked with are highly motivated and educated, yet when they confront certain people problems, they can't easily rely on algorithms and established management strategies to provide clear solutions. And so they can become vulnerable to what we call *spending traps*—where spending, whether it's through money, time, energy, or other resources, comes to substitute for the real work of leading, managing, and executing. The strategies in this book allow you to escape such traps and transform your vexing people problems with solutions you can apply yourself through the skills you already have as a manager.

Let's begin by looking at how thorny problems—like those confronting Sandeep—emerge, grow, and explode, causing people to fall into spending traps. In trying to understand how managers navigate these impasses, we've identified three key insights: First, *people* problems, not *technical* problems, exact the greatest toll on productivity. Second, managers often squander thousands of dollars every day in lost opportunities, aimless meetings, and squabbling teams without realizing or tracking these losses. Finally, most managers in impasse aren't paralyzed in inaction. They are in fact engaged in constant action, but that action is ineffectual, failing to produce rewarding outcomes.

Something Wicked This Way Comes

When you ask most people what a "hard problem" is, their first response typically involves computational challenges in math or chess, or technical engineering issues. However, these are the very types of problems that managers can often solve with their intelligence, training, and analytic models.

Instead, at the heart of most apparently intractable problems at work, we usually find people problems. These might include the colleague with the enormous ego and toxic personality, the team with inefficient decision-making processes, an employee who is unmotivated to change, and all the resulting conflicts that emerge from these human dynamics. It is these predicaments—not the technical enigmas—that ultimately become the deepest time sinks and money pits that managers face, precisely because they seem impossible to correct through coherent methodologies and analytics.

Wicked problems are a class of *truly* challenging problems—such as climate change, terrorism, and the health-care and pension crises. The word *wicked* does not refer to their good or evil nature, but rather to their deviously impenetrable structures.[4] Because people problems have wicked features, conventional approaches do not allow managers to appreciate their complexity, and may, in fact, lead to wasteful and ineffectual strategies for solving them.

Of course, managers never get a memo or an e-mail that clearly announces that a wicked problem is brewing in their organization. But there are at least four cardinal characteristics by which we can recognize the wicked problems that can ensnare us.[5] And Sandeep's people problem met all the criteria.

One feature of wicked problems is that they lack a neat formula for resolution. With more technical or logistical problems, we can rely on established algorithms to work through the issues. But people problems such as Sandeep's always involve unique individuals with complex issues and concerns that can't simply be modeled and resolved through linear problem solving. Wicked problems do not have "owner's manuals."

A second key feature is the lack of demonstrable answers. Ordinary problems, such as "What is 240 divided by 6?" or "What is the price/earnings ratio of our acquisition target?" have clear, verifiable answers. However, the people problems that keep managers up at night have no go-to answer key. Instead, there are multiple possible strategies that they need to work through, and there is no single best answer—indeed, often there are no conclusive solutions whatsoever. And in many cases, truly wicked problems cannot be solved; at best, they can be tamed.

Another feature of wicked problems is that it is often impossible to test proposed solutions. When you're dealing with people, testing different solutions is risky because those tests could have irreversible consequences. In Sandeep's case, if a new strategy caused certain members of the team to become angry and frustrated, the situation might devolve irretrievably.

Finally, wicked problems contain complex interdependencies to multiple problems. Sandeep's team was embedded in a complex, global, cross-functional network, so any action would create ripple effects. The two ringleaders were of course linked to others, so if Sandeep antagonized them, he would lose the rest of the network, multiplying the problems. People problems leave little room for error, so one impulsive move can cost you dearly.

As we'll see, the managers and leaders who are most effective at managing wicked problems are those who—rather than fixating on the conventional solutions that initially come to mind—actively shape these problems and then identify a diverse range of options to combat the issue.

The Hidden Waste of People Problems

When managers think about people problems, they often picture small-scale inefficiencies—arguments with coworkers, unproductive teams, disorganized meetings, and unmotivated employees. By contrast, when they think about issues in finance, marketing, and operations, they mention high-level issues that could rise to the CEO's desk.

In our work with organizations, we have observed that while managers might be personally frugal and careful in the financial aspects of their operations, they unconsciously tolerate significant waste with respect to their people problems. Managers like Sandeep are often stunned when they discover the value being erased by the "small-scale" issues. People problems typically become the largest money pits at work, and they grow without the organization's awareness because the true costs of this class of problems typically aren't measured. Because such problems are not readily quantified in the way that, say, capital expenditures are, we became interested in trying to calculate the everyday value destruction they trigger. In addition to quantifying the waste, we also hoped to develop methods to escape these money pits that capitalized on ideas, not invoices.

What's in Your Garbage Can?

A popular TV commercial has the tagline, "What's in your wallet?" We became interested in finding out what is in managers' *garbage cans*—whether it's wasted money, time, knowledge, or other resources. To quantify the waste from people problems, we developed a survey called the Daily Waste Score.

We asked the eighty-three executives who spoke to us about their most critical impasses to put a price on the amount their companies lost each day due to a range of "small-scale" people issues like interpersonal conflicts and unproductive weekly staff meetings. We gave them a number of prompts and asked them to estimate the daily costs, on a scale of $0 to $20,000, of each. Figure 1-1 shows the results of our findings. (You can calculate your own Daily Waste Score by filling out the chart at the end of this chapter.)

We expected our study to reveal significant waste. However, we were not ready for the magnitude of the results. We were expecting a tremor and we witnessed an earthquake!

Bottom line: In the course of a day, the executives estimated wasting an average of $7,227.07 per line item per day, for a total of $144,541.30 per day, summing each of the twenty points of waste. That's an astounding $52,757,574 of lost value and potential per year per organization on "small-scale" people problems. Again, these are perceptions rather than scientific measures, but they reveal the significant value that could be captured by addressing these issues.

FIGURE 1-1

Results of the Daily Waste Score survey

Average amount executives estimated they wasted per day on each item on a $0–$20,000 scale.

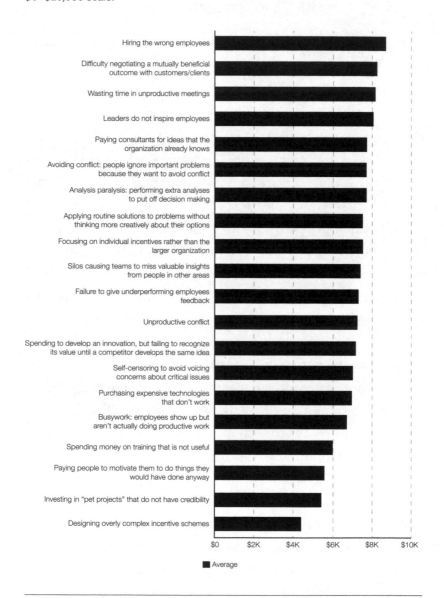

■ Average

The Two Types of Waste

The losses calculated through this survey can be classified into two different types of waste.[6] *Type I* waste is readily discernible and easily quantifiable in immediate financial losses. Consider the following example: In 2005, former French president Jacques Chirac unveiled Airbus's plans for a double-decker jet, the A380, in a glittering party that celebrated both European integration and technological advancement. However, at that very moment, Airbus engineers were already in firefighting mode, caught in a crisis that would belie both claims; cost the company over $6 billion in materials, labor, and multimillion dollar fines for delayed delivery; and ultimately send the parent company's stock tumbling over 26 percent.[7]

The ostensible reason for the delay was a software compatibility problem. The German factory delivered hundreds of miles of cable that failed to fit the planes on the assembly lines in Toulouse, France. (To appreciate the complexity: each plane required 100,000 different wires, for a total of 330 miles per plane.) But underneath this apparently technical problem, there were layers of wicked people problems. The French head of the A380 program had unsuccessfully tried to persuade the German designers to update their software to integrate it companywide. In the words of a senior Airbus executive, "It was partly a question of national pride. The German engineers sort of felt that there was a French solution being imposed on them. But the fact was there was a tool being used in Hamburg that was behind the times."[8] And at the top, the rivalries between the French and German leadership personified the company's decades-long efforts to integrate the British, Spanish, German, and French manufacturers into a single company.

Even though these underlying people problems directly cost the company over six billion dollars in Type I waste, it also created *Type II* waste—the indirect costs—which can be even more dangerous, as the losses often accumulate covertly. Type II waste does not come with a yellow memo, a purchase order, and an invoice. It involves the pervasive spending that Sandeep could quantify only by opening up his calendar and estimating meeting length, attendees, and agendas—everyday value destruction in terms of hours lost to interruption, stress from unproductive conflict, squandered ideas, and countless other metrics that often do not make it onto the profit and loss statement. For Airbus, the Type II waste included the hours employees spent and the stress they experienced as they engaged in the firefighting efforts. Type II waste also included lost opportunities, such as the multibillion-dollar deal with Singapore Airlines that Airbus lost to a competitor. And an even more invisible form of Type II waste involved the projects that could not be initiated because of the resources diverted to fixing the mess. This type of invisible waste often goes undetected for years in organizations.

While tales of corruption and corporate greed dominate the headlines, this daily hemorrhaging of money due to people problems doesn't even make a back page story, though it is often far more expensive. For example, in one study, US employees reported spending 2.8 hours per week dealing with conflict, amounting to approximately $359 billion in paid hours, or the equivalent of 385 million working days in the country as a whole. Further, 25 percent of employees said that avoiding conflict led to sickness or absence from work, and nearly 10 percent reported that workplace conflict led to project failure. And over one-third of respondents said that conflict alone resulted in someone leaving the company, either through firing or quitting, leading to intellectual property losses and time and money spent replacing the employee.[9] These costs reveal just some of the ways people problems produce Type II waste.[10]

Our point is *not* that managers should resist making important investments in their businesses and people. As educators and consultants ourselves, we believe that spending in the name of problem solving and employee development can often add real value to the bottom line. Indeed, managers can waste by *not* investing in areas that offer significant returns. This book, however, specifically focuses on the *wasteful* spending that represents everyday value destruction at work. These are the places where people are spending a lot (in terms of both time and money) and getting very little return for it. By recognizing where these instances occur, you can start to finally fix the issues.[11]

Action without Traction

When people think about frustrating situations such as Sandeep's, they often equate impasse with *inaction*. However, recall that only 20 percent of the managers in our sample reported that their organizations were doing "basically nothing" with respect to the critical impasse they faced. The other 80 percent were caught in a frenzy of action— but unfortunately, it was action without traction. They were treading water, expending considerable energy to get nowhere.

Many highly effective people, among them the types of executives who tend to be charged with handling the organization's toughest problems, are vulnerable to action without traction precisely because they tend to have *active* rather than *passive* approaches to problems. That is, they've embraced the idea that good management involves action and they are thus unlikely to wait passively for the situation to resolve itself. Like Sandeep, they are smart, open-minded, action-oriented, and quick to try new things. These aptitudes paradoxically also make them vulnerable to spending their time, money, and energy on actions that may not produce results.

The problem, as we will see, is that of *misdirected* action. To use a metaphor from engineering, managers have to capture and transmit meaningful *signals*, while screening out and reducing transmission of *noise*. As applied to problem solving, the signals represent the cues that are valid and meaningful, and the noise involves irrelevant cues.

When people focus on the noise or fail to transmit true signals with high fidelity, they find themselves in action without traction. Their actions do not translate into desired consequences because they are transmitting noise (and producing waste) rather than operating from signals (and adding value).

How do managers lose the signal? When people in organizations face complex problems, their rational processes begin to disintegrate and they start reaching into what organizational researchers describe as the "garbage can." What this means is that, even though formal meetings may have an appearance of rationality, for example, what's actually happening is that the actors, problems, and possible solutions are in fact swirling about in a chaotic and noisy fashion—and decisions emerge as the different pieces of garbage that come together somewhat randomly.[12] When managers reach for a solution, they're frustrated as they find themselves capturing noise rather than meaningful signals. Here's why.

THEY HAVE THE WRONG MENTAL MODEL. In complex situations where people grasp for solutions haphazardly, the root problem is that they lack an accurate understanding of the situation—making it impossible to parse the signal from the noise. Many managers and leaders have a story that they tell themselves and others that explains the situation in cause-and-effect terms—their mental model of the situation. They fixate on particular signals and assume that these translate into specific consequences through a particular process. But often, these mental models may not be entirely accurate.

Consider an everyday behavior that reveals how the wrong mental model leads to action without traction. If you ask people how they make their house warmer in the winter, they will tell you that they turn up the thermostat. Fair enough. However, most people turn up their thermostat really high—way past their desired comfort zone—because they're implicitly operating from a mental model that views the thermostat like a car's gas pedal.[13] The higher the temperature setting, the faster they think it will heat the house. But thermostats don't work like gas pedals. If you want to heat your house to 70 degrees, setting a thermostat to 70 degrees will heat the house just as quickly as setting it on 85 degrees. Small changes in how they set the thermostat or simply using a programmable thermostat to set the thermostat back even seven degrees could knock about 21 percent off monthly energy bills according to studies.[14] With the wrong mental model of the problem, people lose touch with the signal and their actions are wasteful and ineffectual.

THEY CHANGE COURSE TOO QUICKLY. When managers discover that the solution they picked may not be working, they quickly move to another. But this merely leads them to a different kind of action without traction: they frenetically retrieve other solutions from the garbage can without exploiting them sufficiently. They risk falling into what's known as a *failure trap*—the vicious cycle of trying a solution, receiving negative feedback on it, and quickly moving on to the next "fix" with similar exuberance.[15] Managers who take the time to learn from a failed solution are able to distinguish between the noise and the signal—and discern the right signals moving forward.

THEY FIND SUBSTITUTE PROBLEMS. When it becomes difficult to find reliable signals with respect to wicked problems, sometimes people stop searching for solutions and instead unconsciously find different problems instead. The *substitution principle* is the psychological process by which people replace a tough problem with an easier one.[16] People facing hard problems sometimes fixate on substitute problems that may be easier to act on, losing touch with the real problems.

For example, every ninety days, your organization may require everyone to change their passwords to protect the systems from data breaches and hacking attempts. So everyone racks their brains to create new passwords. But is this action, however purposeful it feels, actually solving the true problem of making the account more secure?[17]

According to security expert Bruce Schneier, the password-changing guideline was based on a traditional assumption that the attacker is a stealthy eavesdropper. Changing your password frequently is an effective strategy to defend against someone who has discovered your password and lies in wait. This narrowly defined type of hacker may be relevant if you are a celebrity likely to be stalked by the paparazzi or a national security operative vulnerable to espionage. But simply changing a password is useless against a broader range of security problems (e.g., someone who guesses your password, then immediately uses it to steal money from your bank account).[18]

What's worse, Schneier has found that the substitute problem and solution trigger a new, unintended problem. When people must change their passwords frequently, they are more likely to select combinations that are easier to remember (and for others to guess) than if they were allowed to keep the same password. So although it seems like more action is better, these substitute actions create the *illusion of progress* while failing to address the true problem—and perhaps even making it worse. Not only does fixating on the noise lead to purposeless action, it also creates counterproductive action.

THEY ASSOCIATE NEW PROBLEMS WITH OLD SOLUTIONS. When managers reach into the garbage can, they also often retrieve past problems and their solutions. They know what has worked before, so they tend to use those same solutions again. But this is akin to using a hammer to fix every household issue. The solution sometimes produces results, but at other times, people are left pounding away with an ineffective hammer that fails to nail down the true problems but leaves them feeling exhausted from the wasted effort.

––––––––––––

For action-oriented people, the challenge doesn't lie in being more motivated to solve a wicked problem; it lies in capturing and transmitting high-fidelity signals—regaining the connection between their actions and the consequences. Wicked problems lead to waste when people invest time and money in actions based on an incomplete or incorrect understanding of their causes, or when they use tools that worked in the past and that happened to rise to the top of the garbage can. To restore the link between purposeful action and desired consequences, managers have to reexamine their mental models of common but vexing business problems, explore different solutions, and measure whether they actually work.

The Five Spending Traps

In our work as researchers, consultants, and teachers, we studied how business leaders such as Sandeep choose to spend their time and allocate their resources to solve their most intractable people problems, and how much time and money is unaccounted for, even under the watchful eye of corporate accounting. And we discovered systematic patterns of wasteful spending that can trap managers as they face off against these problems.

To understand the specific motivations that underlie wasteful spending, we asked over a thousand management and executive students to identify instances of waste in their organizations. We read their stories and discovered that, nearly without exception, the problems could be attributed to one of five distinct spending traps, which reflect processes by which people either fixate on the wrong signals or fail to transmit meaningful signals, transforming their well-intentioned action into misdirected action.

We were also struck by one commonality. These spending traps did not emerge from people's weakness, lack of expertise, or character flaws but were often the direct result of many of the talents and skills that had allowed them to excel in so many other situations. When overused and misapplied, these behaviors—which were typically signals that led them to value—entrapped them. We will see how managerial strengths gone wild—expert knowledge, competitive spirit, compassion, and communication and delegation skills—can ensnare you in spending traps. We'll then consider how to manage and channel your strengths to access real solutions.

The Expertise Trap

Psychologists studying chess masters learned that it takes about ten thousand hours to become expert.[19] This holds true for mastery of almost every skill—music, athletics, or leadership, to name a few. As experts in their particular domain, managers usually know what to do automatically and without a second thought, and it usually works. This may save time and energy, but it also means that managers are prone to put tasks on autopilot. If they fly into the uncharted territory of novel problems in these moments, they may catapult straight into the Expertise Trap—the block people face when their well-learned defaults in handling earlier situations prevent them from capturing signals in novel situations.

To see how expert behaviors can lead to entrapment, let's consider that great American pastime: dieting. Most people would like to think that they can control how much they eat. However, people struggle to control their food intake precisely because they are expert eaters. People don't need to stop and think about how to eat, they eat multiple times a day and can do so with their minds off. And that's the problem.

In 2005, psychology researchers at Cornell University created a special dining table in their lab. When diners entered the "restaurant," they were served a steaming bowl of soup. However, unbeknownst to the diners, this bowl was connected to hidden pipes that slowly refilled the bowl as they ate. It was truly a bottomless bowl. The researchers were interested in how much the diners would eat if the bowl never became empty. The result? Most diners binged, eating 73 percent more soup when served from self-refilling bowls.[20] The diners ate mindlessly, relying on convenient but false external signals (like an emptying bowl) and losing track of the true signal: whether or not they were actually hungry. When people are practiced at an action, they turn their minds off. In such situations, the Expertise Trap causes people to lose touch with their inner compass and its conscious, attentive awareness that guides them to true signals.

Expertise arms people with tried-and-true strategies that can be applied in relevant situations, but it can also narrow attention. As people start down a particular problem-solving path, their focus narrows to particular signals and tunes out the noise. This is adaptive and functional—if they've zeroed in on the true signal.

But sometimes what seems like noise is actually a signal that people should pay attention to. And sometimes what automatically seems to be the signal is in fact just noise. When people fixate on faulty signals, they direct their action to false problems. This leads to action without traction, as they end up having the same tiresome conversations, repeating sequences of behavior, and exploring conventional solutions.

In chapter 2, we explore the Expertise Trap in depth—how people rapidly form patterns as they encounter novel and uncertain situations, how they structure these patterns and often miss the big picture, and the dangers of barreling toward problem solving too quickly. We will explore how to mindfully deploy and check your expertise—and stop spending on well-worn patterns, frames, and solutions that might have been successful in the past but are no longer effective. By engaging in problem *finding* before problem *solving*, you can control and shape problems, and see innovative solutions that can break through impasse.[21]

The Winner's Trap

The Winner's Trap results from the fact that most successful managers and the talent they work with are, well . . . successful. They have all gotten to where they are in their jobs and careers by prevailing in competitive situations, whether it's clinching the interview, getting promoted, or succeeding in the marketplace; they are, in essence, winners. But most winners seldom like getting out of their comfort zones. And for them, the zone of maximum discomfort is losing. When we talk to self-described winners, the most common thing we hear from them is *not* how much they love winning; it's that they find losing excruciating.

What we have observed, however, is that winning at problem solving involves getting comfortable with a set of skills that people tend to associate with losing—questioning their identities as winners, acknowledging that it is nearly impossible to always be right, and learning to accept losses and change course. In many organizations, people get trapped in a fruitless course of action because staying the course is rewarded, whereas failing, learning, and accepting losses are not.

Another disquieting reality is that the rival in the next office could be a source of high-value insight. Individuals, especially winners, often turn a blind eye to ideas, solutions, and best practices that are not their own, and particularly if they come from competitors in the same organization. Who wants to be labeled as the follower rather than the leader? But managers who shut out these ideas miss high-value signals that could allow them traction on their toughest problems.

The Winner's Trap also affects people because they want to look good in others' eyes. For instance, when innovators and project leaders invest resources trying to salvage a failing project, rather than accept the sunk costs, this isn't just about being selfish and competitive. Admitting that much time and money has been squandered on a failure is a tough pill to swallow, and it's natural to try and save face in front of peers and bosses. And winners, who are preoccupied with avoiding losses, are especially vulnerable.

Although a competitive drive propels people to be creative, unique, and successful, it can lead to counterproductive action as people act at cross-purposes and create lose-lose outcomes for everyone involved.[22] Chapter 3 describes various underlying reasons that organizations pit self-interest against social interest and trigger the Winner's Trap. By redirecting these innate tendencies to win and also impress others, managers can channel their people's competitive spirit into value creation rather than waste production.

The Agreement Trap

The Agreement Trap is the opposite of the Winner's Trap. It emerges when people avoid transmitting negative signals to others so as to not threaten existing relationships. Rather than speaking honestly and confronting problems head-on, those caught in the Agreement Trap are overly concerned with being collegial team players and end up avoiding necessary conflicts. In an effort to spare other people's feelings, managers get trapped in misdirected action whereby they dance around issues instead of getting to the heart of the problem.

Why do so many people avoid conflict? People assume that others are much more fragile than they actually are. Most of the managers and leaders who we studied described themselves as thick-skinned, but viewed others as thin-skinned.[23] By underestimating their peers' ability to accept negative messages, people capitulate in negotiations even when it doesn't make sense. They make premature concessions when they should hold their ground. They give feedback but distort the signal in confusing or vague communications. These problems are often exacerbated in "politically correct" conversations that tiptoe around sensitive topics such as race and gender. The result is that people may have access to high-fidelity signals, but fail to transmit them clearly to those who need to receive them.

When people avoid conflict, they lose opportunities for the insights and breakthroughs that often emerge from disagreement. In some cases, creating a workplace tolerant of dissonance doesn't just improve the way people work and save money, it may also be the difference between life and death. For example, in hospitals where nurses did not feel comfortable when offering crucial but potentially threatening information to their superiors, there were more fatal mistakes.[24]

In chapter 4, we discuss the Agreement Trap in detail and offer strategies that balance managerial compassion with the courage to negotiate instead of capitulating to employees' demands, fearing conflict, or avoiding issues due to political correctness. We also discuss how stimulating issue-based conflict—rather than interpersonal conflict—gives your team the mental and social exercise to build stronger, smarter ideas.[25]

The Communication Trap

If the Agreement Trap is about how silence and under-communication keeps people from getting to the heart of the problem, the Communication Trap is about noisy overcommunication that gets people no closer to the high-fidelity signals and real traction on problems. To be sure, lack of communication is the source of many problems, and leaders must often open up the lines of communication between people. But *more* communication isn't necessarily *better* communication. Increasingly, managers are losing the ability to communicate with discretion and priority, creating talk and noise around their problems rather than purposeful actions to address them.[26]

In our over-networked world, you'd think communication problems would be solved already. But paradoxically, the very technologies that are meant to help people communicate can lure them into the Communication Trap. The vast amount of data and information managers get—and even ask for—can make for ineffective discussions and misguided decisions. The information revolution may have increased the amount and speed of communication, but it hasn't improved the quality of communication and people's ability to understand each other.[27]

And the sheer quantity of communications is staggering. According to one study, the average employee spends 40 percent of the workweek reading and responding to internal e-mails. That's the same as spending all day Monday and Tuesday in meetings and only beginning to work on real problems on Wednesday.[28] Curiously, people are more likely to e-mail others the closer they are geographically.[29] So, even as technologies theoretically make it possible to communicate instantly across the globe, they're still communicating with people nearby who are similar and familiar—and who therefore expose them to similar and familiar solutions—rather than more novel insights.

To develop an escape route from the Communication Trap, we asked hundreds of managers about the situations in which they've been able to capture critical ideas at work. We learned that their high-signal interactions did not occur via e-mail, at corporate networking events, brainstorming sessions, or office parties. Rather, they cropped up in unplanned, spontaneous interactions—lunch breaks, unexpected social encounters, even bathroom breaks. Each of these allowed diverse people—who would never have *chosen* to interact—to come together, creating the conditions for unexpected fusion to occur. Unfortunately, as we'll discuss, such interactions between diverse people are becoming increasingly rare.

In chapter 5, we explore how managers can overcome the Communication Trap by creating new interaction patterns that allow them to venture outside of their silos and connect with people beyond the similar and familiar. We show how managers can create randomness by design and set the stage for people to capture high-value, novel signals without expensive new technologies. At the same time, we also describe best practices that discipline information search so that diverse signals do not descend into chaotic noise.

The Macromanagement Trap

We've all heard of micromanagers, who hover over their employees and control their every move. They have excessive attention to detail with little or no regard for the autonomy of their employees. Macromanagement is micromanagement's lesser known, but extremely costly, opposite. Managers fall into the Macromanagement Trap when they fail to pay sufficient attention to details, often in the name of empowerment and delegation. They create teams, committees, and task forces to solve problems, expecting them to spontaneously create value and synergy, without establishing the conditions to make that happen or stepping in when there are challenges.[30]

When a signal encounters an opening or free space, it breaks down and spreads in different directions. In the same way, when a macromanager creates a vacuum by failing to structure the group adequately, the result is an uncoordinated, directionless team that flounders and fails. This hands-off approach to group interaction and problem solving leads to unfocused action, creating more breakdowns than breakthroughs.

For instance, when we observed a high-level team's meeting about defining a new strategy, we saw how an understructured interaction could quickly descend into waste. There were eight attendees, who were aware we were there to observe. After the meeting, we asked them separately what percent of the total talking they did—making comments, asking questions, offering opinions—during the meeting. Most people estimated they did about 12 percent of the talking, which would be about right if everyone contributed equally. However, we had been tracking and timing all comments and had calculated that two alpha members accounted for over 60 percent of the talking!

In unstructured meetings, certain people control the airwaves while others mindlessly assume that their mere physical presence constitutes a contribution. One of the most high-risk zones for waste production occurs when the biggest talkers in your group also offer the least substance; that is, they emit noise without generating meaningful signals. And worse, that noise drowns out meaningful signals from more knowledgeable participants.

If you lead an unstructured group meeting, you are essentially conducting an orchestra where members each play what they please, whenever they please—the result is noise, rather than a harmonious symphony. In chapter 6, we will describe specific techniques to design group interactions that maximize your likelihood of locating meaningful signals within the group, while cutting down on the noise. These include several ready-to-implement strategies to create the connective tissue that coordinates group interaction so that the right people can speak at the right times and for the right length of time. We reveal how groups can gain better awareness of their processes through *metacognition*, whereby the mere act of explaining or describing how one makes decisions induces a new awareness and improves coordination capabilities.[31] You'll learn how, by training people together, you can improve not just individual skills and talents, but also ensure that people learn those skills in context so that they cohere as a team.[32] Finally, to escape the trap of marathon meetings, inefficient committees, and unnecessary face time, we'll show you how to design interactions that iterate between the "cave" and the "commons" to gain the power of both focused individual time and collaborative interaction.

Conclusion

As you face off against your toughest people problems, five key traps can leave you stalled in action without traction: the Expertise Trap, the Winner's Trap, the Agreement Trap, the Communication Trap, and the Macromanagement Trap. All of them initially masquerade as promising signals that play to your strengths—your knowledge, competitive spirit, and likeability and your drive to communicate with and empower others. But they can also lead you to spend your time and money in noisy alleys full of garbage where you cannot make headway on your problems.

Many people do not realize that they're losing value through these traps because they're trained to focus on the direct, easily quantifiable costs, blinding them to the indirect costs. But at this moment, when turning profits is harder than ever, managers are taking a new look at their workplaces and assessing how they spend and where they waste. Now more than ever, there is no room for investing in the noise rather than the signal.

As you read about each of the traps, think about which ones lurk in your organization. Perhaps it's just one, or maybe you find yourself struggling with multiple traps at once, as Sandeep did. In either case, you need a plan of attack to stop spending time and money in these sinkholes, break out of the impasse, and solve your most frustrating, wicked problems.

The focus in this book is thus on helping you recognize and access your potential as a leader, tame your talents, and also capitalize on the untapped resources within your organization. Because there are often thousands of complex decisions and small-scale interactions that can create large-scale waste at work, the strategies we've outlined are, by design, fine-grained, specific, and practical. We hope many of them provide you with a set of ideas to implement with your team. In fact, you may have already heard of some of these tools before and even used them on occasion. Used in the right way and in the right context, these strategies can free you from the traps that can ensnare the best of us. Let's begin.

Calculate Your Daily Waste Score

You can identify what problems are costing you the most—not only in money—but in time, energy, and additional resources. By monitoring these costs, you can see not only the enormity of the waste in your organization, but you can target areas to improve.

For each prompt below, estimate how many dollars per day are lost, factoring in not only things you're billed for (like hiring consultants or additional talent) but also those indirect costs (lost time, resources, and opportunity costs). How much money does your organization lose each day due to the following people problems that you or another member of your team face? Select a number from $0 to $20,000.

1. Failing to reach a mutually beneficial negotiation with customers/clients. $_____

2. Having unproductive conflicts. $_____

3. Purchasing expensive technologies that don't work. $_____

4. Applying the same solutions to every problem, without thinking more creatively about other options. $_____

5. Performing extra data analyses because people won't make decisions. $_____

6. Paying consultants for ideas that the organization already knows. $_____

7. Spending money developing an innovation, but failing to recognize its value until a competitor develops the same idea. $_____

8. Investing in "pet projects" that do not have credibility. $_____

9. Focusing on individual incentives rather than the larger organization. $_____

10. Self-censoring or avoiding voicing concerns about critical issues. $_____

11. Ignoring important problems to avoid conflict. $_____

12. Hiring the wrong employees. $_____

13. Failing to give underperforming employees feedback. $_____

14. Living in silos and missing valuable insights from people in other areas. $_____

15. Wasting time in unproductive meetings. $_____

16. Prioritizing face time and doing unproductive busywork. $_____

17. Spending money on training that is not useful. $_____

18. Paying people to motivate them to do things they would have done anyway. $_____

19. Designing overly complex incentive schemes. $_____

20. Failing to inspire employees. $_____

Add all your numbers up to see your final balance. Now, look at which prompts have the highest price tag. Keep these areas in mind as you read through the following chapters. The advice in this book aims to help you get rid of these costs once and for all.

CHAPTER 2

The Expertise Trap

Brooke is a top collections agent at her call center. Her job is to ensure that customers who have fallen behind on their accounts get onto repayment plans. Even though the call center has pages of scripts that help less experienced agents communicate, Brooke doesn't rely on a script. Rather, she thinks like a chess player, quickly assessing the situation and directing the conversation to accomplish her goal.

However, Brooke's expertise failed her when she called Alex about a repayment plan. Alex opened the call by describing a major complication in his cancer treatment. Brooke quickly responded, "I'm so sorry to hear that," and then stepped right into collections mode. Alex was infuriated by her response and hung up, though not before berating her and threatening to call her supervisor. Brooke called back quickly, but Alex didn't answer, and the account eventually became delinquent, costing the company thousands of dollars. Thus, in a matter of seconds, Brooke was jolted out of her routine and a standard call became explosive.

Brooke had years of experience, but experience wasn't her friend in this situation. When Brooke reflected on what happened that day, she explained that she had slipped into autopilot. She had heard Alex's words, but she had not really processed their meaning, which would have required her to step outside her usual routine.

Expertise has many attractive benefits, often allowing people to effortlessly exercise excellent judgment and achieve success. For example, just as most people don't need to think about how to tie their shoes or ride a bike, expert tennis players don't have to think about how high to toss the ball when they serve because their muscle memory is sufficient. In the same way, leaders may not have to think when they hold a task force meeting or look at a balance sheet. They have performed these tasks thousands of times.

When experts place these well-learned behaviors on autopilot, they can conserve mental resources for their more pressing obligations and complex problems. Nobel laureate Herbert Simon referred to these shortcut thinking strategies as *satisficing*, a blend of *suffice* and *satisfy*.[1] Satisficing means settling for what is good enough. It is the opposite of *optimizing*, or reaching one's full potential in the situation—being the best. And there's nothing wrong with that. Most people do not have the time to relentlessly search for an optimal outcome in all situations, so it's efficient to move forward with an option that is good enough. This approach to problem solving can economize on time, money, and effort.

That is, until the solutions fail. When managers are flying on autopilot—as Brooke was—they can occasionally get blindsided by the novel, the paradoxical, the wicked, the business-as-unusual situation. Then, they glide straight into the Bermuda Triangle of the Expertise Trap, where well-learned routines that typically serve them so well can backfire.

Consider the patient who walked into a Texas emergency room on September 26, 2014. He presented textbook flu symptoms: some stomach pain and fever. On his chart, one note described his condition as "unremarkable," and another notes that it "was remarkable only for nasal congestion and a runny nose along with mild abdominal tenderness." The nurse even chatted with the patient about his recent, exhausting plane flight from Liberia. However, the world would soon discover that this was no routine stomachache from airsickness or flu. Thomas Eric Duncan was America's first Ebola patient. Because everyone in the emergency room was following the same routinized script, Duncan was discharged, rather than being treated and isolated, raising the risk of spreading the disease in a large urban setting. Duncan died within days, leaving behind two nurses fighting for their lives and a hospital reeling with lawsuits and questions about its preparedness.[2]

Tanya's father is a pediatrician, and he often describes his job as diagnosing routine ear infections and colds 99 percent of the time—and life-threatening conditions 1 percent of the time. What makes medicine so hard is that you can't simply go on autopilot, because you never know whether you are facing the 1 percent case—the signal in the noise. This observation applies not just to medicine, but to most areas of work and life as well.

People get traction on their actions when their mental models cleanly parse true signals and screen out the noise.

And experts have powerful mental models that allow them to be highly sensitive in parsing signals from noise most of the time. But when experts over-apply the patterns, routines, and experiences that they've learned over years of practice, they can miss novel signals. They might also fixate on noise when interpreting a new situation if that noise had been a relevant signal in prior situations.

The question, then, is: How can managers break out of the Expertise Trap while not throwing away all of the knowledge, experience, and insight that allow them to be effective in most situations? It would certainly be inefficient for you to put yourself on a new learning curve every day, as if you were a novice. The answer lies in three critical skills that allow you to shift from automatic to manual mode:

- Pattern recognition and tests of disconfirmation: Sometimes people assume that a current situation will perfectly match a pattern they've found typically useful in the past. To reduce the error rate from these deficient mental models, generate "tests of disconfirmation" to see what you don't expect to see—but need to see.

- Seeing the figure and the ground: As people rapidly structure a situation, their expertise helps them quickly determine what is relevant and what isn't. But, sometimes what seems to be the important signal isn't, and what's seemingly just noise is actually essential to solving the problem. The challenge lies in seeing both the *figure* (the issue at hand) and the *ground* (the larger context) simultaneously to widen the lens to capture signals that might otherwise be missed.

- Problem finding versus problem solving: Once people frame problems based on their past experiences, they tend to fixate on familiar patterns and approaches, and dismiss others. To "un-fixate" and see new patterns, a problem-finding approach challenges you to see the problem from multiple angles and collect broad data, not just what fits into a narrow frame—again loosening the pattern and capturing signals that would otherwise go unnoticed.[3]

Now let's consider each of these strategies that help you to escape the Expertise Trap by deploying your experience and knowledge purposively.

Patterns: Detect and Check

Humans are natural pattern finders, seeing faces in the moon and images of mythical creatures in the stars. Patterns allow people to feel in control of uncertain situations. When people feel that they lack control over their environments, they begin to search for patterns.[4] Specifically, they are more likely to believe in superstitions and conspiracy theories and even see patterns in random scribbles. Tanya and her colleagues, organizational researchers Cindy Wang and Jennifer Whitson, found that these moments of control loss caused both Singaporean Chinese and Americans to search for prediction through horoscopes.[5]

Patterns are useful because they organize noise. Think of noise as a random collection of signals. Randomness is useless for the most part. So pattern making is a powerful skill, allowing people to find signals in noise, clarity and regularities in confusion, discern cause and effect, and ultimately, predict the future. But, when people see faces in the moon and animals in the stars, they commit the statistical error of *overfitting*—that is, organizing what is in fact noise into a pattern.

Experts are particularly incisive in seeing patterns where others can't, and in turning noise into clarity. As an example, look at the picture below. Now shut this book and try to draw it.

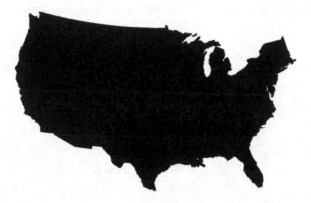

If you are American, you would most likely be able to reproduce the drawing more rapidly and accurately than if you were Chinese, South African, or Norwegian.

Now look at the image below, shut the book, and try to draw it:

This is hardly the most complex character in Chinese writing, but it would take concentrated effort for someone who was not familiar with that language to draw it after one glance. An expert speaker of Chinese, however, would instantly be able to reproduce this character for *scold*, just as Americans could recognize and reproduce the map outline of the United States.[6]

But here's the problem: Sometimes you don't see what you think you see. Look again at the image you just drew of the United States. Did you draw in the state of Maine or notice that much of Maine was missing from the image above? If you did not notice this, it's because once you have a pattern in mind, you switch to autopilot and ignore the details in the actual situation. This is called *top-down perception*; the pattern is now what's guiding what you see.

Patterns render noisy environments into clear, predictable, meaningful signals. But when people form mental models based on illusory patterns, it can cost them dearly. Let's consider a very common business example of how pattern-fixation sets the trap for some costly (but avoidable) management problems.

The Price of Illusory Patterns

Chris was six-foot-four, with wavy salt and pepper hair. He wore perfectly tailored European suits, and spoke with a deep, resonant voice. According to the executives who had hired him, Chris was the complete package: he had worked for similar companies and had top university credentials. But most importantly, they could "connect" with him. People had good feelings about him immediately; some even mentioned that he could be CEO material. However, Chris was riding on charm alone. His subordinates were the first to realize that, as good as his high-level comments sounded at those initial meetings, he had large gaps in technical knowledge. As the "halo" of his "leadership look" evaporated, Chris quickly lost credibility with the talented employees he was supposed to manage.

When people see the bad fits around their own office, they often wonder how those individuals came to be hired in the first place. Just ask a few colleagues about their interview technique, and they'll often reveal that they went on instinct: "I knew in the first five seconds that s/he was right for the job," or "I don't even need to look at a résumé. I use my gut!" Some firms openly admit to putting away the résumé when interviewing people.[7]

But while intuition sometimes guides people to the right decisions, these shoot-from-the-hip judgments can also lead to expensive failures—costing organizations hundreds of thousands of dollars in lost money, time, and resources. The executives who completed the Daily Waste Score estimated the cost of bad hires as $8,697.67 per day (or $3,174,659.55 in a year); of the twenty items in the survey, this was the largest point of waste cited. In expert calculations, the cost of a single bad hire—a second-level manager who earns $62,000 per year and is terminated after 2.5 years—is $840,000, or over thirteen times his or her salary. That's because the true cost includes hiring costs, cost of maintaining the employee, severance, and Type II costs such as the consequences of disruption, mistakes, failures, and missed business opportunities.[8]

How do people fall into this spending trap? In many ways, their instantaneous assumptions about what makes for a good manager can operate like ancient horoscopes, allowing them to form patterns about people and make predictions about their personalities and their future potential without sufficient empirical data to support those conclusions (e.g., tall people are more authoritative, good-looking people are nicer). Few people would openly declare that they prefer to hire physically attractive candidates, the problem is that these stereotypes infiltrate decision making unconsciously, the assumptions morph into "facts," and create a distorted reality.

The problem isn't that people form patterns—the problem is that people accept those patterns without testing them. Organizational researchers Jeffrey Pfeffer and Robert Sutton made the striking but chilling observation that "if doctors practiced medicine the way many companies practice management, there would be far more sick and dead patients, and many more doctors would be in jail."[9] In response, they called for evidence-based management; that is, subjecting first impressions, gut feelings, and intuitions to rigorous testing. Think of all those interviewers who proudly swear by their intuition. Have they actually checked how effective their intuition is, compared with other methods? How many successful employees have they hired, relative to those who didn't work out? And how many great candidates did they miss? In the spirit of Galileo Galilei's appeal to "Measure what is measurable, and make measurable what is not so," evidence-based management calls on managers to use scientific methods to collect and analyze data on their major decisions so they can learn from their actions and improve their decision making over the long term. Let's consider three approaches to ask the questions and collect the data that make it easier to parse the signal from the noise.

CHALLENGE THE PATTERN. Suppose you're presented with the following sequence of numbers: 2, 4, and 6. Your task is to guess the rule that governs the pattern. To determine the rule, you'll have to identify the next three numbers in the sequence. Most likely, you would think "ascending consecutive even numbers," and generate a sequence such as, "8, 10, 12." And you would be right. So, now you're pretty much certain that the rule you have in mind is correct. Except, it's not. There are actually a number of sequences where these three numbers appear: numbers divisible by two, whole numbers, or numbers less than 10. This is because the actual rule for this particular example is simply, "Ascending numbers." So, you could have picked, 7, 29, 144.5 and also been right.[10]

This exercise reveals the tendency to confirm one's suspicions, rather than challenge them. This tendency is known as the *confirmation* or *myside bias*, and everyone has it.[11] When you challenge the patterns you have in mind through tests of disconfirmation, you can recognize their boundaries and can build more accurate mental models.

So, in the example above, you see the sequence 2, 4, 6 and immediately think 8, 10, 12. Take a moment and ask, "That's my confirmation bias at work, how can I test it?" First, you might try an odd number, and you'd discover that would work also: the numbers are still ascending. Thus your assumption that all numbers would be even is invalidated. Then, you might think, "I assumed that the numbers got larger, what if I tried a smaller number?" You would then discover that smaller numbers violate the rule. With two challenges to your own assumptions, you've learned more specifics about the rule than you thought you knew at the start.

In Chris's case, an interviewer who already had a favorable impression of Chris could confirm that hypothesis by steering the interview such that Chris could cherry-pick highlights of his leadership history. The interviewers can thus unconsciously create self-fulfilling prophecies by behaving more warmly toward preferred candidates but dismissively toward less preferred candidates, leading the interview in a particular direction that ultimately confirms the preconceived expectation.[12] In one study, interviewers who were led to believe a candidate was extroverted tended to ask questions such as, "Tell me about the last party you attended." And when they believed a candidate was introverted, the interviewers asked different questions, which tended to elicit responses that supported that impression, such as, "Tell me about what you do with all the time you spend alone." The candidates essentially faced two different interview situations.[13]

To mindfully expand your powers of observation, intentionally implement tests of disconfirmation. The essential question is apparently simple but psychologically difficult—what test could prove my hypothesis wrong? Rather than assuming Chris was above the bar, this question could have allowed the interviewer to zero in on the specific gaps in Chris's résumé, forcing Chris to prove he was actually above the bar. Or, Chris's interviewer could have directly compared Chris's résumé (absent the picture) to others to test the hypothesis that he was in fact the best for the job.[14] In Sandeep's case, he might have asked himself, "What are the reasons—*other than* the fact that I find the two antagonists so difficult—that my team is struggling to get coordinated?"

PUT UP A CURTAIN. To truly put your patterns to the test, collect data that will prove your intuitions wrong. By actually conducting a test and searching for such information, the bad news (that you were wrong) is in fact good news (now you know what's really going on). By playing the bad cop with yourself, you've improved your odds of averting a spending trap. But here is the challenge: the confirmation bias also skews how people design tests, collect the data, and analyze the results. So, how can you design tests that avoid biases such as the self-fulfilling prophecy to parse the signal from the noise most cleanly?

In the 1970s and 1980s, symphony orchestras in the United States began to scrutinize their heavy overrepresentation of male musicians and the growing concern that major symphony orchestras were not necessarily hiring based on merit. Stated more starkly, it looked like they might be guilty of bias in the selection of talent. So they conducted a rigorous experiment: musicians would no longer audition in full view of the hiring committee, but rather from behind a curtain. Therefore, the only signal emitted was the music itself. The noise—gender, physical appearance, and dress—was concealed. With this simple change, the chance that a woman would advance to the next audition round rose by a shocking 50 percent.[15]

This result warrants serious pause, especially as it pertains to corporate interviews and promotions. To be sure, it is not exactly practical to interview C-suite or even middle-management candidates behind a literal curtain, so what is the managerial equivalent?

To put up your curtain, design a clear and unbiased test of your hypotheses. If you want to screen out the noise of physical appearance, for instance, evaluating candidates via phone interviews could help.

But phone interviews still allow other forms of noise, including gender and accent, to enter. And, one curtain that can help control self-fulfilling prophecies in phone or face-to-face interviews is a *standardized protocol*. Instead of throwing away their scripts, the best interviewers create the same conditions for every interview—they ask everyone the same questions, and even keep their chair the same distance from the candidates.[16]

Finally, check if you're trying to test a hypothesis that's impossible to address with concrete evidence. We often hear that candidates need to be likeable, "fit," and work well with others. Unfortunately, any potential employees whom you "like" based on first impressions can be retrofitted to these nebulous criteria.

And because these criteria are hard to test, people look to how the interviewee talks to draw their inferences—which can be completely invalid signals of their true beliefs and behaviors. Interviews are often designed to select for "smart talk"—as compared to effective action, great teamwork, and deep thought.[17] Chris, for instance, was skilled at smart talk—he always sounded great, even though he was light on substance.

To counter this, the best interviewers assess measurable behaviors. So, if you want someone whose key responsibility is to conduct strategic analysis, then you're much more likely to find a good fit by asking all the candidates to do a strategic analysis of an issue at your company. Then follow up in a biased-free way by comparing each of their reports ("the signal") anonymously—removing name, gender, race, and physical appearance ("the noise").

FIND THE GEMS IN THE DATA MINE. In addition to designing experiments, analyze history. In this age of big data, businesses have gotten comfortable letting the data speak with respect to operational or marketing questions; for example, when managers compare strategies to reduce waste in a fast food chain, or design a marketing intervention for a particular customer segment. But they're less likely to use that rigor with respect to the people problems they grapple with on a regular basis. Whether you want to hire the right employee or assemble the best team, creative opportunities to optimize your choices are right in front of you, by unearthing the unanalyzed data from past experiences.

Psychologist Robyn Dawes, for instance, faced the challenge of selecting successful PhD applicants.[18] Here, as in business, the wrong choice can be a costly decision for any university. While a great PhD student can greatly enhance a faculty member's research, an unproductive student costs the university roughly $100,000 in full tuition and a salary for four years—and that doesn't even include the cost of training the student and missed opportunities to develop a more promising young researcher. To extend his powers of observation, Dawes collected historical data on all the graduate students admitted to the University of Oregon's psychology department from 1964 to 1967, in terms of their grades and GRE test scores. He then had faculty members rate whether the students were outstanding, above average, average, below average, or dropped out of the program due to its academic difficulty—a measure that all faculty members agreed was important. What Dawes discovered was that the best predictor of student success was the students' grades and GRE test scores. Analyzing the dormant data his organization had been collecting on repeated decisions, he had put his intuition to the test to see which factors were truly predictive. Further, he found that human judges rarely—if ever—are able to outperform these models. In fact, his department had not only relied on invalid cues, but they used those invalid cues inconsistently.

How can managers apply Dawes's data analytic techniques to their people problems? For example, suppose you want to better understand how well the teams you manage are working together, so that you can maximize their productivity for an upcoming project. To extend your own powers of observation, create a grid or spreadsheet listing all or many of the teams created over the past several years and the names of the team members. Use a scheme to evaluate as many pieces of information about those situations as you can: the size of the team, its composition, the resources allocated, the nature of the project, and so forth. Next, enter their results: Was the project successful, or was it a complete disaster? What worked well, and where did trouble arise? Compiling these data for the first time can be painful, but keeping updated records like these as part of as part of the HR process creates a running database that continually reveals which teams are working and which are not.

How do the results compare with your expectations? Are there any surprises that you can act on? For example, we often find that many managers expect the most high-performing individuals to comprise the best teams, but that's often not the case (you'll read more about this in chapter 6). By simply paying attention to composition, you might be able to design the collaborative teams you've dreamed of without wasting your effort and money on factors that don't offer predictive power. Using the data from your own organization's past history, you've extended your powers of observation to draw valid inferences about what matters and why.

Dawes argued that almost anything, even random choice, is better than human intuition when it comes to making predictions. One study found that randomly selected leaders could be more effective than elected leaders![19] People often choose leaders on the basis of charisma and charm, which may be great for the cover of *Gentleman's Quarterly*, but not necessarily for actually leading a team.

Dawes even suggested periodically creating a team that you would intuitively expect to fail. This is yet another way to fight confirmation biases. Assemble a group of people for whom you have low expectations—whether it's about their productivity or interpersonal behavior—and test whether those expectations are in fact warranted by the data. Without this disconfirmation test, you can't really know if your model of team design is working. In other words, if you only create groups that are expected to succeed, how would you ever learn if the people you did not expect to succeed would indeed fail? The disconfirmation test will allow you to find value that would otherwise have been missed.

And each of these skills is particularly important when approaching wicked problems. Even though you may not be able to directly test solutions to wicked problems, these tests are still crucial because wicked problems defy obvious formulations— requiring you to get past conventional first impressions about what's causing what.

Seeing the Figure and the Ground

We've explored how people unconsciously rely on patterns that guide their perception in a particular direction, obscure critical details, and create blind spots. Now consider one specific and common type of pattern that can obscure critical signals: focusing on the figure rather than the ground. In other words, fixating on what's front and center can often cause you to miss signals that reside in the background.

Take a look at the following picture. What do you see?

When Americans look at this picture, most focus on the individual fish on the right, the leader (i.e., the *figure*). But when Chinese subjects look at pictures such as these, they're more likely to focus on the school of fish as a whole (i.e., the *ground*), and imagine them chasing that single fish![20]

Tanya and researchers Jessica Sim, Jeanne Fu, Chi-Yue Chiu, and Ying-Yi Hong asked American and Singaporean subjects a different task: to pick the leader. Unsurprisingly, nearly all Americans selected the fish in the front.[21] But, of the Singaporeans, 25 percent said the leader is the fish *in the back*. These different perceptions represent very different expectations on what a leader's vantage point should be. The front leader was looking out at empty space—presumably the future. The back leader, however, had a view of the entire group and a holistic perspective of the situation.

These differences in perspective are pervasive in different cultures, even extending into artistic tastes. North Americans and Western Europeans prefer images where the figure dominates the ground, whereas East Asians prefer pictures with rich contexts. European museums historically favor portraits, while Asian museums have a larger percentage of landscapes.[22]

By forming patterns that focus on the figure, while ignoring the ground, people create a blind spot that can obscure essential signals in the environment. Successful leaders are able to widen the aperture of their managerial camera and consider not just individuals but their whole context. Beyond fish and art, let's consider the implications of seeing figure versus ground patterns when you deal with managerial problems. Think about each of the following situations. Quickly write down your first impression about why the event occurred.

1. You present an update on one of your latest projects. Your coworker is quick to ask questions and criticize details. What's the first reason that comes to mind?

2. Your employee continually asks you for guidance on projects rather than using his/her independent judgment. What's the first reason that comes to mind?

3. The job candidate you're interviewing stumbles through the questions. What's the first reason that comes to mind?

Do any of these first impressions sound familiar?

1. Your coworker is intentionally cutting you down because he is not collegial.

2. Your employee lacks initiative and leadership qualities.

3. The interviewee lacks the experience to do the job.

These are mundane situations that managers face every day—but in absence of conscious thought, they might leap to conclusions without evidence. The tendency to incorrectly attribute behavior to stable and fixed personalities rather than the situation is called the *fundamental attribution error.*[23] Suppose, instead of zeroing in on the person, you attributed these behaviors to temporary, environmental factors. Your explanations might be:

1. Your coworker has been having an awful day and is just irritable.

2. Your employee's past boss was a micromanager who expected to be constantly updated.

3. The job candidate is nervous because it's stressful being in an interview situation.

These latter assumptions aren't fundamental attribution errors— they focus on situations. Indeed, there are multiple potential interpretations of these objective events, each of which leads to a dramatically different story, which in turn affects the approach to managing them. Let's take a look at that first scenario again and consider possible explanations for your coworker's behavior:

You present an update on one of your latest projects. Your coworker is quick to ask questions and criticize your project . . .

. . . because he has poor social skills.

. . . because he feels threatened by your project.

. . . because he is dealing with issues at home.

. . . because he is actually very excited about your ideas and wants to provide feedback to help them succeed.

In each of these examples, assumptions seep into the facts and influence your perceptions of the personalities of the people you're dealing with. When you cement others' behaviors into an unchangeable personality type (e.g., Sandeep's two troublemaking employees are recalcitrant), you miss the true causal "story" that explains their actions. In doing so, you can end up solving the wrong problem. For example, you think that you're dealing with an angry coworker, when in fact he's stressed about a pressing situation. A confrontational approach to that worker could exacerbate his stress and make a bad situation worse.

Because the fundamental attribution error can hijack your understanding of others and their situations, you need a workaround, just like a test of disconfirmation. We call it a *background check*. Obviously, this is not the kind of investigation that an FBI agent might conduct, but it is one that leaders should engage in to take a close look at their perceptions and see the background story they might have missed. This is *not* the well-known rule to ask "why" three times—which can simply lead you into a deeper pit of fundamental attribution errors (e.g., Why did she perform poorly? Because she is lazy. Why is she lazy? Because she lacks proper work ethic. Why does she lack proper work ethic? Because that's how she was raised. And so on.).

Before digging deeper into one specific "why," use the background check to reveal a broader range of possible "whys" that could underlie the person's behavior.[24] To loosen your assumptions, ask: What factors, other than this person's personality, could be responsible for their behavior—A difficult task or situation? Luck? Their effort or their approach?[25] How has this person behaved in past situations? How have other people behaved in similar situations?[26] How might this person's personality and their situation interact to produce a particular outcome? How might your own behavior have affected the situation?

The last question is the most difficult to answer honestly. People enjoy playing a starring role in their personal dramas, but as the hero, not the villain. So they naturally ascribe causes for others' behaviors that make them feel good about the role they played in creating the outcome, and avoid those that can cast a less than flattering light on their own roles.

Perhaps the "whys" at the heart of *your* contribution to the three situations described before include:

1. Your coworker criticizes your project because the project has serious flaws that should be discussed openly.

2. Your employee is asking for regular guidance because you were unclear in describing the project and expectations up front.

3. The job applicant stumbles because your tone and style of asking the interview questions flustered him.

With an increasingly global workforce, our research has also explored how different cultures explain these conflicts through different stories. For example, while East Asians are more likely to pay attention to the background, Tanya's research with Michael Morris, Chi-Yue Chiu, and Ying-Yi Hong indicates that they are more likely to fixate on and blame the group and its "personality."[27] On multicultural, global teams such as Sandeep's, this means that people problems can rapidly polarize into group problems based on generalizations about particular national groups or specializations. So, recognizing this cultural habit, East Asians can also widen their perspectives by thinking about other possible causes—beyond the level of the group— that could offer them a richer understanding of the situation. By filling in their team's or their culture's usual blind spots, managers can assess more accurately the situation they're facing and respond accordingly.

Problem Finding before Problem Solving

One cardinal feature of expertise is the ease with which possible solutions can be brought to mind. But, when facing wicked problems that require a broader search for options, people can find themselves constrained in an iron cage of their own mental models and patterns. As you gain more expertise, your thinking can become more rigid because you rapidly rule out interpretations that do not fit the expected patterns. Most of the time, this cognitive skill allows you to parse signals from noise, but it can also shut out novel ways to see problems.

Consider one example of how a lack of expertise can actually open the door to new and novel solutions to stubborn problems. Two environmental engineering students in Africa, Moctar Dembélé and Gérard Nyondiko, observed that the most dangerous animal in the world was not a lion or a shark, but the tiny mosquito. Malaria, spread by mosquitoes, kills more than 400 thousand people annually, and is the leading cause of death in sub-Saharan Africa. UNICEF estimates that malaria costs Africa "$12 billion every year in lost GDP, even though it could be controlled for a fraction of that."[28] Of course, a fraction of $12 billion is still a lot of money. One report, authored by experts from the United Nations, World Bank, and drug companies, recommended that governments and NGOs should budget $5 billion annually for malaria prevention, compared to the $1 billion currently spent, with an additional $9 billion in research and development over the next decade.[29]

And in spite of all that spending, people have little traction on the problem. In particular, mosquito repellents are often ineffective because they are expensive, toxic, and require disciplined use.

On the one hand, people know the solution to the problem of malaria: protect against mosquito bites. But in reality, they haven't focused on "finding" the underlying problem accurately: how to design broadly safe and effective mosquito repellents that local people are likely to adopt. Dembélé and Nyondiko then wondered: Why not embed the repellent in soap? Their product, Faso Soap, which naturally repels mosquitoes without dangerous chemicals, won Berkeley's Haas School's 2013 Global Social Venture Competition.[30] Instead of requiring expensive medical personnel or behavioral change programs, the soap, which costs 59 cents a bar, fits within locals' normal hygiene routines and could save thousands of dollars in medical expenses for every malaria case it prevents.

As non-experts, Dembélé and Nyondiko approached the problem from the ground up, without top-down, conventional solutions. They didn't institute complex, expensive programs that would complicate people's lives; instead, they developed a solution that could enter into people's everyday routines.

This creative step involves overcoming what's known as the *pre-utilization bias*, a cognitive block that occurs when people have used a tool or resource in a particular way in the past, making it nearly impossible to use it in a different way.

To see how pre-utilization might lead to the Expertise Trap, consider psychologist Karl Duncker's problem-solving experiments. Duncker handed people a box of matches, a box of thumbtacks, and a box of candles and asked them to mount a candle vertically on a nearby wall to serve as a lamp. Less than half of the people were able to solve this problem.[31]

However, when people received the same supplies but with the matches, tacks, and candles outside of their original containers, they suddenly saw the box as part of the solution, not just a container to hold supplies, and were able to come up with the solution. The literally "outside-the-box" solution is to mount a candle on top of a box by melting wax onto the box and sticking the candle to it and then tacking the box to the wall. By simply presenting the resources to people in a new way, Duncker was able to transform the functionally fixed problem solver into a creative innovator.

The problem of disease in the developing world is an example of an intractable, wicked problem where proposed solutions typically take the form of million-dollar programs that are extremely difficult to implement. But it also reveals the possibility to manage even complex problems with simple "one cent solutions."

Practicing the Problem-Finding Approach

To practice the problem-finding approach, Sandeep led his team of managers through a series of challenging conversations that helped loosen their fixed assumptions.

ASK A NEW SET OF QUESTIONS. Sandeep knew that each of his previous discussions had degenerated into a "garbage can" group dynamic. That is, people got fixated on their own particular solutions and they advocated just those. People weren't listening to or learning from each other. And they couldn't get past the blame: the automatic "why" stories led to highly charged discussions where fundamental attribution errors flew back and forth.

To turn the garbage can into a vault, we coached Sandeep to help the group break out of the patterns they were fixated on. Rather than structuring the discussion so that people simply tossed around their pet solutions, we instead asked him to have them take a step back and answer the following set of questions (anonymously) to help articulate their mental models of the changes in their competitive environment: *Where* is it happening? *When* did it start? *Who* is involved? *Why* it is happening? *How* is it happening? *How much* is happening? and *What* is happening?

As Sandeep read the write-ups before the group's next meeting, he could clearly see how people (and indeed coalitions) were attached to distinctive solutions and were seeing very different problems. Behind each of their strategies were different mental models about the "where," "when," "who," "why," "how," "how much," and "what."

But when Sandeep shared people's write-ups with the group, he was surprised that the discussion began with comments about the significant areas of agreement. By allowing people to thoughtfully articulate their mental models of the problem in writing, people were able to process more deeply than if they'd just thrown around first impressions at a meeting. In short, the iron cage was being rattled, and beginning to open.

To push his team even harder to consider other perspectives on the problem, he divided the group into subgroups, assigning the technical folks to write about the problem from the marketing perspective, and the marketing team to write about it from the technical perspective.

And then he asked them to write from other perspectives: the user's, the CEO's, and their key competitor's.

By challenging the team to see different problems (instead of brainstorming solutions), Sandeep could finally lead a discussion where people weren't wasting time talking past each other, defending their own solutions, and poking holes in others' solutions.

ILLUSTRATE DIFFERENT POINTS OF VIEW. We then coached Sandeep to divide the team into three subgroups, each of which broke down the coalitions by including both marketing and technical team members. Each team was charged with developing a drawing or physical model that could visually represent their complex interdependencies and relationships.

Because wicked problems are complex and abstract, the teams were asked to make them more comprehensible by concretizing them—that is, visually representing them using actual objects and prototypes. This is analogous to how an abacus uses a concrete apparatus to represent abstract math. Math education in Asia has relied on the abacus for thousands of years, allowing children to see and even touch numbers. In the same way, the teams benefited from a concrete representation—drawing the problem—instead of just talking about it.[32]

Through these initial conversations, the marketing side began to recognize that they had to prioritize deep-level causes rather than focusing on solutions that offered only a short-term boost. The key for them was to take a step back to see the problem from multiple perspectives—instead of narrowing in on their preconceived solutions.

You can do your own visual exercise with your team to better understand what assumptions are at play and to get them communicating. Start with a table that lists each team member's name, followed by columns labeled "problems," "solutions," and "resources" (see table 2-1). Have individual team members fill out the table, defining perceptions of the problems, the solutions they see, and the potential resources that need to be involved.

Once everyone has had the opportunity to fill out the table, you'll have a side-by-side comparison of everyone's point of view. You'll be able to note where attitudes differ with respect to the issues at hand, where individuals get fixated on specific solutions, and what resources you'll need to move forward. You'll likely have a wide range of problems and solutions—and that's okay. The point is to get the differences of opinion out in the open, so you can communicate more effectively.

TABLE 2-1

Problem-finding worksheet

People	Problems	Solutions	Resources

Once you're able to see the differences in perspective, discuss them. Ask the following problem-finding questions to guide your team:

- What is the problem?

- How do other groups see the problem differently?

- What are the "where," "when," "who," "why," "how," "how much," and "what" being assumed in each perspective?

- What data supports these different views of the problem?

- How did people come to a particular view of the problem? Self-interest, past experience, underlying analogies?

- Which constituents' needs are missing from these frames, and how might thinking from their perspectives lead to new problem frames?

- Which views of the problem could be integrated to create a more complete view of the problem? Which views of the problem should be prioritized?

- Are there different analogies that could provide new problem frames?

- Can you identify potential untapped resources?

- Can you generate potential one-cent solutions?

In visualizing the differing perspectives and then discussing them openly, you might discover that the problem you were originally aiming to solve isn't the right one. Once that's acknowledged, you can move forward with a solution that best tackles the issues you're addressing, thus breaking the cycle of action without traction.

Conclusion

Most managers have reached a level of expertise in their chosen domain that allows them to accomplish highly complex tasks almost automatically. However, this chapter reveals how depth of knowledge can sometimes lead to the Expertise Trap. People's confidence in situations means they're occasionally too trigger-happy: Ready! Fire! *Then* aim. Without the right targets or signals, this produces misdirected action despite the best of intentions.

Three sets of strategies help you to shift from automatic to manual and manage these tradeoffs. First, recognize the patterns, and then check them. Next, break the habit of focusing on one piece of the puzzle, thereby missing the rest of the picture. Finally, loosen the tendency to get fixated on particular problem definitions, so you can find better solutions that work. Rapid pattern formation leads to erroneous or incomplete mental models of the situation, and it constrains options in problem solving. By recognizing the limits of the patterns and mental models that underlie your expertise, you can find the hidden signals that widen your understanding of people and their situations, and offer you traction in dealing with them.

CHAPTER 3

The Winner's Trap

Americans spend an average of thirty-eight hours a year sitting in traffic (for urban drivers, it's over sixty hours a year) at a cost of $121 billion in lost productivity and extra fuel. Ants, on the other hand, don't have traffic jams. Entomologists have tried to create ant congestion by narrowing their paths and blocking their movements. But ants always collectively solve the problem by signaling the optimal paths to their group and continuing their steady march forward. Why are ants so much better at avoiding traffic jams? The answer lies in the fact that ants don't have a sense of self and exist only as cooperators in a collective.[1]

The Winner's Trap makes people look at traffic, and much of human interaction, as a zero-sum game of winners and losers. Of course, people want to win. They convince themselves that if they drive more aggressively, look for the fastest lane, and pass drivers slowing them down, that they'll beat the traffic.

In fact, the constant jostling for first place, aggregated across the thousands of cars on the highway, actually slows down traffic for everyone as cars stop and start and accidents cause total gridlock. A recent study on driverless cars found that substituting only 10 percent of cars on the road with driverless cars, which take the ego out of driving, would save a thousand lives and $38 billion dollars in avoided accidents and gridlock.[2]

To be sure, a competitive spirit drives people to persist, be creative, become leaders, and win at work.[3] Metaphors of business as war, sport, and dog-eat-dog survival are ubiquitous in business. But there is a downside: when people bring the Winner's Trap mindset to tasks that aren't best solved with competition, they fail to get traction on their action because they are working at cross purposes with others rather than acting in concert.

Organizational Traffic Jams

Perhaps you've found yourself in an organizational traffic jam at work. For example, Sandeep's team was gridlocked because people refused to share the lane and work toward a common goal. Maybe people on your team block each other as they clamor for finite resources, attention, and opportunities, or you're championing an innovation that is stuck in the slow lane. Our research has focused on the *traffic of ideas* in organizations and the frequent and wasteful gridlock that occurs when ideas fail to spread to those who need them—and indeed, often disappear entirely into black holes. While ants emit trail pheromones that clearly signal a food source to other members of their collective, humans following the trail of good ideas in their organizations often find weak signals, jammed networks, and failed transmission. Former Hewlett-Packard CEO Lew Platt famously bemoaned this waste, noting, "If only HP knew what HP knows, we would be three times more productive."

Tanya and Sally Blount (professor and dean of Kellogg School of Management) were interested in understanding how the Winner's Trap creates an environment where people miss high-value signals from colleagues. We sought to answer one question: do people pay more attention to the *merit* of an idea or the *messenger* of that idea?[4] And more to the point, how do people react to ideas generated by talented insiders?

Most people would like to think that they don't judge a book by its cover and that they can evaluate an idea on its merits alone. However, people consciously (and unconsciously) promote or devalue the ideas of certain messengers. The type of messenger we became particularly interested in was the *internal rival*—a person within the organization with whom people feel competitive. In particular, we wanted to know how much waste results from ignoring a rival's vault of ideas.

We were both passionate about the subject of competition because of our own experiences in competitive sports. Tanya played competitive tennis through high school and in college. Leigh was a national and an international champion in masters cycling. A key idea that inspired this research was one that we learned through hours of practice: sharpening your competitive abilities is not only about fine-tuning your individual technical skills or even about just "trying harder." The path to fundamental improvement lies in exposing yourself to strong competitors who may be better than you, being willing to accept the pain of a loss, and using those experiences to learn and improve.

Consider tennis superstar Serena Williams. Even though she did not compete as often as others in tournaments as she grew up, she had the daily luxury (and pain) of being exposed to an older, stronger competitor in her big sister Venus, who served her with many hard losses as she developed her skills. In our own research, we have studied managers who are similarly surrounded by undeniable internal talent. The question we asked was, when do they embrace that talent and use it to raise their own game and when do they avoid learning from it?

Tanya and Jeffrey Pfeffer observed how managers shut out the ideas of talented insiders in a case study of Fresh Choice, a trendy West Coast salad buffet chain.[5] Facing a stale concept and a sinking stock price in the 1990s, its managers had an eye on a small, quirky competitor chain from Seattle called Zoopa. Zoopa had hit on a creative and lively design. Instead of the usual salad buffet line, it created an international farmers' market, with open kitchens and vendors at separate, colorful food stations energetically engaging customers. Zoopa became an inspiration, and Fresh Choice adopted ideas from Zoopa's menu offerings, restaurant design, human resources practices, and service initiatives to invigorate its concept. Fresh Choice eventually decided to acquire three of the four Zoopa restaurants for $6 million in 1997. This move wasn't about simply expanding their physical assets and getting some new recipes. Fresh Choice wanted to acquire Zoopa's human assets and the intangible knowledge, creativity, and energy that came with them.

But, after a brief honeymoon, Fresh Choice managers started derogating Zoopa's model, which they'd once openly admired. The very people Fresh Choice managers had once described as "bright," "creative," and "energetic" were now described as "burnt out" and "sloppy." When Zoopa's key top managers resigned, the intellectual capital and intangibles that Fresh Choice had hoped to gain vanished. After spending millions of dollars to buy the business and months to integrate the two companies, Fresh Choice was left with only the physical assets. In 2012, after filing for a few bankruptcies, Fresh Choice shuttered its remaining restaurants.

It's true that Fresh Choice faced a number of the typical challenges after an acquisition, but we also saw that the Winner's Trap caused people to squander the knowledge right in front of them. Paradoxically, it seemed that it was harder to learn from Zoopa managers once they were coworkers instead of competitors.

To test whether people might feel particularly threatened by an insider's ideas, Leigh and Tanya, along with Dr. Hoon Seok Choi, developed a protocol that allowed us to examine envy in terms of actual behavior. We first asked managers across a number of different businesses to think about a rival within their own organization or a rival in a competitor company.[6] Next, we asked them to make hypothetical, high-stakes business decisions about an idea generated by that person and whether they were willing to learn from that rival. Finally, we asked them how much they would invest in learning from the rival's ideas (using a $10,000 budget).

The results were surprising and sobering. Managers who believed that the idea came from an internal rival were *less* interested in learning from that person and allocated only $1,740 toward learning from them. Managers who thought that the same idea came from an external rival allocated $2,470. That is, they were willing to pay 42 percent more to an outsider for the exact same idea!

We immediately turned our attention to the question of why managers were less interested in the internal rival's ideas. When we asked participants how much status they'd lose by adopting the ideas, the managers considering the ideas of internal rivals anticipated losing 36 percent more status than those who learned of external rivals' ideas. In other words, learning from the internal rival felt much more like losing. So, to avoid a loss in status, they preferred espionage against a competitor to collaboration with a colleague. The Winner's Trap was at play.

These findings also explain why managers might be so receptive to signals from consultants. Like competitors, consultants are part of another organization, so they don't compete directly for internal opportunities, making it less threatening to affirm their expertise. Indeed, as consultants ourselves, we have benefited from the bias that organizations and leaders have toward outsider information. It's sometimes easier to take a hit to the wallet than a hit to the ego.

So, how can people extricate themselves from the Winner's Trap without losing their competitive edge? The first key is for their managers to be clear about when competition is valued and when cooperation is valued.

Doublespeak about Cooperation and Competition

Teams find themselves in traffic jams because the lines on the business road are often unclear. In Tanya's work with researchers Oliver Sheldon and Adam Galinsky, she found that people became confused and disturbed when they dealt with "frenemies"—people who straddle the line between friend and foe.[7] Indeed, people were more likely to avoid disliked competitors who complimented them, thus setting up an ambiguous relationship, than those who made an insulting remark that clearly demarcated that line.[8]

Leaders and managers can also unintentionally blur these lines when they claim to value cooperation while in fact rewarding competitive behaviors. To address this, we asked Sandeep to measure the various situations in which his team operated as if they were playing a zero-sum game—that is, viewing a colleague's win as a personal loss. During one meeting, we counted how often people referenced their peers' ideas and built on them (statements such as, "As Amy just mentioned . . . " or "Building on Brian's idea . . . "). We discovered that group members tended to give credit to those ideas whose owner would help them succeed in the long run. During the course of the ninety-minute meeting, *every* referential statement cited someone in the same geographical region, an indication that people were hesitant to cross silos and let another internal team's idea be validated. In other companies, we've observed different patterns—for example, people referencing only their higher-status colleagues and failing to build up ideas of lower- or equal-status colleagues.

Ask an observer to sit in on one of your own team meetings to quantify whether conversations are about establishing winners and losers instead of building collaboratively. To delve into this micro-level observation even further, also count conversational teardowns: Who gets interrupted? Whose ideas are appropriated or recycled in the conversation without acknowledgment? Whose ideas become conversational dead-ends (not developed or followed up)? And whose ideas are directly dismissed? This is a fast way to observe and quantify competitive rather than collaborative dynamics as people exchange ideas.

When we shared this data with Sandeep, he felt frustrated, given the amount of time he had spent emphasizing teamwork and collaboration. Why was it so hard to get people on board with that message?

We then asked Sandeep the even more difficult question: Was collaboration actually valued and rewarded? When we showed him the names of the people who tended to speak most in the meeting and were most likely to display divisive conversational patterns, Sandeep admitted that not only were those individuals highly respected ringleaders of their respective cliques, but that he himself had given them more airtime at meetings, and more attention and power at work. Despite all the lip service, competitive power plays trumped collaboration at every turn. Even though Sandeep said "cooperate," the unspoken incentives in play said "compete."

Tanya and Jeffrey Pfeffer's research revealed how organizations place managers in a bind with respect to learning from their peers. When executives conducted hypothetical performance evaluations of two similar managers—one who'd learned information from an external competitor and the other who'd learned from an internal competitor—they rated the former 21 percent higher on creativity, 18 percent higher on competence, and as expending 17 percent more effort. As a result, they were 16 percent more likely to promote the external learner and gave him a 35 percent higher bonus.[9] These incentives encourage people to chase expensive ideas from outside competitors (which seems more creative and resourceful) instead of learning from their own colleagues (which seems unoriginal).

Organizational researcher Steve Kerr named this misalignment the "folly of rewarding A, when hoping for B."[10] For instance, a manager who rewards "attendance" rather than "productivity" or "quality," spends money to finance behavior that is at odds with the team's true goals. The manager gets face time without any guarantees that employees will use that time to be more productive. Or, salespeople may be told to focus on customer service while the company rewards only sales, leading to highly aggressive behavior designed to make a quick sale that upsets the customer. Unsurprisingly, employees will generally work only for what's actually rewarded.

Or, consider the carefully-designed incentive plans that are the standard in sports today. They seem like smart economics, aligning individual behavior with clear performance goals. As just one example, former National Football League player Terrell Owens ("T.O."), a six-time Pro Bowl wide receiver, signed a contract with the Cincinnati Bengals in 2010 with $2 million in base salary and an additional $2 million in financial incentives if he achieved various quantified targets. If he made 60 catches, 900 yards, and 10 touchdowns, he would enjoy a $333,333 payday. He'd get another $333,333 if he delivered 100 catches, 1,300 yards and 14 touchdowns for the season.[11] However, whereas few questioned T.O.'s personal talent or his effort, some questioned his team orientation, wondering whether the famously self-promoting receiver needed any more incentives to focus on his own statistics.

Even though incentive packages such as these attempt to carefully balance individual performance with team incentives, such worries are well founded. Former NFL player Dave Meggyesy observes that these incentives still focus players on individual payouts at the expense of their team's success:

> I was confronted with the dilemma of whether or not to share [insight about an opponent] with the other

linebackers. Coaches constantly talk about team spirit but I've always wondered how the hell there can be team spirit if I know that the more other linebackers screw up, the more I'll be able to play, and the more I play, the more money I make. Owners keep writing contracts with performance clauses . . . though these can only work to create divisiveness on the team . . . [12]

Players become so distracted by trying to make their individual numbers that they can lose track of the bigger picture: delivering a win for the team.

Even subtle language can create mixed messages about what's valued.[13] For instance, American companies spend $14 billion a year on "leadership training," which often focuses people on themselves and their personal power rather than on being a collaborative follower.[14] And *innovation* is a near-sacred buzzword in organizations, where the "lone inventor" (often labeled an "Edison" or an "Einstein") is synonymous with genius. Some organizations recognize and make efforts to counteract these tendencies. British Petroleum (now BP), for example, awarded a "Thief of the Year" honor to managers who recognized and borrowed good ideas from their peers.[15]

Many managers and business people face a landscape of complex micro-incentives—just like an NFL player's—where jobs are broken down into pieces and employees lose track of the big picture. Even when human resource consultants design incentive schemes that reward team outcomes more than individual results, job responsibilities are complex, making it challenging to specify every aspect of the work that needs to be done. Thus, rather than focusing employees on "winning" the largest share of the bonus pool, the question is how to build a team where people are willing to collaborate. To design a playing field where the players think beyond zero-sum games, one answer lies in allowing people to compete, but creating different paths to win.

Getting Past Zero-Sum Comparisons

Winners are highly sensitive not only to their own performance, but also the performance of their rivals.[16] Just as Serena and Venus inspired each other, such comparisons can motivate people to improve. Sometimes, however, people don't seek a "win" by learning from and outperforming a rival. At Fresh Choice and Zoopa, for example, they were instead tempted to ignore and denigrate the rival—and squander opportunities to learn and sharpen their competitive skills.[17] We wanted to find a way out of this trap.

We noticed a critical relationship in our studies: the more threatened and insecure people felt, the more they tended to derogate successful colleagues.[18] This allowed us to create unique situations that would mitigate threats, so that people could overcome that initial envy and appreciate others' achievements. In one investigation, we asked participants to evaluate their rival's ideas. But before they did so, we asked half of the participants to list a few of their accomplishments or cherished values, then to think about the value on the list that was least personally important, and finally to write two or three sentences about why this value might be important to them.[19] They could think about their own talents in art, music, sports, and social skills, or qualities such as beauty.

The other half were also asked to list values, but in addition, they were asked to to elaborate why these values might be important to *another* person. They weren't reminded of their own achievements at all. So what happened? Reminding managers of their own achievements allowed them to find their more generous selves—indeed, they allocated 60 percent more time to learning about their rival's ideas than the group that was told to think only of others. Even a few minutes a day on this exercise, multiplied over fifteen people on a team, starts a shift to cooperation. The bottom line is, when managers take stock of their own talents and strengths, they're more likely to put each competitive situation in a larger perspective and appreciate others' contributions.[20]

This study also suggests an additional reason why *financial* incentives can set the Winner's Trap in motion: competition for cash tends to be a zero-sum game where there aren't opportunities for multiple winners to emerge. Everyone wants a share of the compensation pool, and a dollar for one is, by definition, a loss for everyone else. If people can be prompted to think about other types of resources, this also helps to create a playing field with multiple ways to win.

There is no doubt that money takes center stage in negotiation and compensation; however, people exhibit a double standard: they assume that *others* are motivated by money and extrinsic rewards—while seeing *themselves* as motivated by loftier, more intrinsic goals (such as having meaningful work).[21] This double standard can wreak havoc on how managers design the playing field. Reducing other people's motivations to just money, we encourage a zero-sum race to claim the largest possible share of the pie (not to mention spending a hefty amount on the incentives themselves).

Other Forms of Motivation

To think more broadly about what resources, beyond money, can motivate people, think about different types of resources. *Resources* are defined as anything that can be transmitted from person to person, and money is only one example.[22] Other resources include love (e.g., affection, good will), services (e.g., babysitting, consulting), goods (e.g., a car or jewelry), information (e.g., knowledge about how to do work), and status (e.g., recognition for achievement).

So, if you invite a coworker to dinner, that person could respond with love ("I'd enjoy being with you again."), services ("I'll cook you dinner next time."), goods ("Here is a gift to show my appreciation."), money ("Here is $40 to compensate you for the cost of the dinner."), information ("Let me share some information about a new opportunity at work."), or status ("You're a great leader at work.").[23]

Each of these six resources can be viewed as symbolic versus concrete, and general versus person-specific. Money, goods, and services represent concrete exchanges, whereas love, information, and status are more symbolic. Resources may be exchanged in a way that is general (e.g., money can be exchanged with anyone without being degraded) or particular (e.g., love is person-specific).[24]

As a manager, it is tempting to focus on the concrete and the general—money and material rewards to the exclusion of the symbolic and personal. When managers overvalue resources that are concrete and impersonal, such as money and material exchanges, they undervalue resources that are more abstract and personalized, such as information, networks, and social relationships. Money tends to dominate all other resources because it allows for quick transactions and it can be recognized across diverse people. To be sure giving money is far easier than extending empathy or good will.

Non-monetary-based resources offer a unique power. When people rely on financial exchanges, it undermines social relationships. Simply put, money makes people more likely to play and work alone, distance themselves physically from others, and avoid helping or being helped.[25] People paid an hourly wage also are less happy and are more impatient in their leisure time because they are more likely to equate time with money.[26] And when law students take their first jobs and are exposed to the practice of billing time, they become less inclined to volunteer.[27] In all of these findings, organizational practices that communicate that "time is money" create spillovers into other interpersonal spaces.

Here is a case in point: We spoke with a manager who described an internal peer recognition program at her company called RAVE (Recognizing and Valuing Employees). Each "RAVE" was a note from one employee recognizing the work of another and a nominal gift card (the nominator could choose a $5, $10, $15, $20, or $25 reward). Because these notes were posted on a bulletin board in the middle of the workspace, she observed, "It became apparent really fast who was doing good work and who wasn't by the repeat RAVEs, and this publicity motivated others to work toward RAVEs rather than the fiscal reward." The cash awards were very small, so people didn't see the money as important. Indeed, we'd argue that such a program would be even more powerful if it offered relational rewards (e.g., a free lunch together). At other companies we've worked for, key rewards have included being selected to participate on strategic task forces, investments in career development, and networking opportunities. These forms of recognition can cost the company some financial investment— but they offer employees a resource that's far more meaningful than a cash transaction.

TAKE MONEY OFF THE TABLE. What would happen if you eliminated individual financial incentives altogether? Wouldn't employees just become opportunistic slackers? When Jay Porter, the owner of The Linkery Restaurant in San Diego, applied a uniform 18 percent service charge to the tab (which was lower than the restaurant's average tip), he discovered a surprising answer to these questions. Without the financial incentive, service did not decline, and in fact, it actually improved![28]

According to Porter, tipping actually distracted his employees from doing their work. In theory, such financial incentives should focus people *more* on the aspects of work managers are rewarding—in this case, bigger tips should incent servers to be more attentive and efficient. But in reality, the servers were constantly being interrupted by real-time compensation feedback (i.e., what they were "winning" and "losing"), which distracted them from focusing on the actual service. Imagine how you would feel if your customers or boss tipped you after each action. Although receiving feedback is important for people, too much feedback actually creates an interference effect.

Porter also observed that the diners who felt offended by the no-tip system worried about how they could punish bad service, while of course claiming that they normally tipped more than 18 percent. Even though these patrons had gained better food and service, they still felt uncomfortable. Porter reminded them they could still complain to management if they ever felt that they were getting subpar service. What they had "lost" was control—the power to use their wallets to exact rewards and punishment.

This sense of control is exactly why managers who vest their power in financial incentives rely on them even when they are as counterproductive as our examples suggest. Managers might get hauled into HR if they use brute force to control employees, but although economic control in the form of rewards, financial incentives, and bonuses can be just as heavy-handed, it carries the more respectable veneer of rigorous economic analysis.

The key point of this example is *not* that people don't need incentives or any structure to their work. Eliminating incentives worked because Porter tapped into resources beyond money. In addition to offering his employees a higher guaranteed wage, he also offered them a job they liked, and trust in their ability to do their jobs without feeling controlled by the power of the wallet.

KEEP PURPOSE FRONT AND CENTER. While competition and incentives can certainly motivate, organizational researcher Adam Grant offered employees at a university call center something more than a financial gain.[29] These employees were soliciting alumni donations, and rather than adding yet another performance metric or contest to win, Grant simply asked scholarship recipients to visit the call center once. One group of agents heard the recipients describe how those donations had impacted their lives by allowing them the opportunity to receive an education. This intervention had nothing to do with financial rewards—it simply allowed call center employees to see that their work had purpose. But "purpose" had financial implications: agents increased their average call time by 142 percent and raised 171 percent more funds, while the group that hadn't been visited by the scholarship student exhibited no change. Employees elevated performance when Grant filled in the gaps in terms of meaning rather than money.

———————

In each of these examples, people could compete and excel without feeling that their success was dependent on someone else's failure.

Refereeing the Game

As people navigate collaboration with their teammates, people sometimes also seek wins by claiming more and contributing less. So sometimes, the competitive lines get drawn *within* teams rather than between teams, and jams emerge as people contribute in self-interested ways rather than cooperating freely.

Even though people try to be fair and reasonable in thinking about what they should give and get, Leigh's research with Max Bazerman and George Loewenstein showed how they also exhibit *creeping self-interest*, and their own sense of entitlement influences their decisions.[30] One example of creeping self-interest emerged when researchers David Messick and Keith Sentis studied how two groups—one that worked long hours with moderate productivity and one that work short hours with high productivity—remunerated themselves. Both groups overpaid themselves and underpaid the other. When asked to justify their decision, the low-productivity group stressed the time they put in, while the high-productivity group focused on what they got done.[31] Everyone had a yardstick scored with their own self-serving metrics, which sustained their sense of entitlement, leading them to see a "fair" outcome as the one that allowed them the greatest share of the resources.

We asked Sandeep to clearly show his two contentious subgroups the extent that they were contributing to different end goals for the team as a whole. While people readily focus on what others *take* from the group, they are often less aware of what others *contribute*.

Let's make this personal. Suppose you and your significant other are individually asked to evaluate the percentage of time that each of you does household chores: doing the dishes, laundry, taking out the trash, etc. When researchers asked married couples to complete this task, they discovered that, the totals frequently added up to more than 100 percent. This, of course cannot be true, unless people are biased to see themselves as carrying significantly more weight in the joint responsibilities of marriage.[32] The reason is not just that people believe that they contribute more, but also that they fail to recognize the efforts and contributions of others. Married people remember each moment that they themselves spent scouring the dishes in vivid detail—but cannot know each time that their spouse did the dishes as well.

When Sandeep began sharing more information about different people's contributions to the group as a whole, team members started to gain a better appreciation of the big picture. They still pulled out their own personal yardsticks to measure contributions, but they were more realistic about their own claims because they better recognized what others had contributed. Beyond sharing information about contributions, we'll explore next how you can use your team to self-police those members who seek wins by giving less and taking more.

Publicize versus Hide

Every semester, our MBA students complain about free riders in their project groups—people who game the system by trying to ride the team's coattails while contributing as little as possible. In fact, free riding is the most commonly reported management problem we hear about in groups, teams, and committees. Fortunately, there is a strategy you can implement to curb free riding on your teams.

Maria was a senior engineer leading a team of computer programmers. Her team would meet their deadlines, but their code was often full of errors. She told us: "I've got to catch the errors, point them out, and then deal with their egos when they get defensive. I've got no time or patience for this. I don't want to be micromanaging them, and I wish I'd hired more careful people in the first place."

As she thought through her predicament, many complex and costly solutions came to mind. Her first impulse was to micromanage the team, but that left her frustrated. Another option was to fire the entire team and hire more careful and experienced (and therefore more expensive) engineers. Alternatively, she might invest in training so that her programmers would produce cleaner code. Or, she could hire other managers to help her police the team. Another possibility might be to hire a consultant to analyze their work and reorganize it. All of these solutions required money, time, and stressful reorganizations.

As we observed Maria and her team, we learned that she had made the team's project deadlines public, which motivated them to get their work done on time. However, she evaluated individual members in private and gave them the critical feedback behind closed doors.

At first glance, it appears that Maria set up the situation just right, following the accepted management best practice of praising in public and punishing in private. But by following this practice, Maria failed to tap into a valuable source of social influence: the power of publicity. To activate the power of publicity, begin by discussing responsibilities publicly and asking your team to agree to these obligations in front of others. People who make a public commitment or pledge are more likely to feel accountable and follow through. They have committed to a *psychological contract*, which is why people often believe handshakes and verbal agreements to be as binding as written contracts.[33] And when public radio stations announce the name of people who pledge during fundraisers, it makes it harder to skip out on the pledge. But you don't even need to broadcast people's names to society at large to make people feel accountable. In work with researcher Catherine Shea, Tanya discovered that when people simply wrote down the names of people close to them, they were less likely to lie, cheat, or engage in antisocial behavior.[34] In other words, just thinking of a group to which you feel accountable will prompt you to behave in a more socially responsible manner.

We advised Maria to shine the social spotlight on free riders by creating public situations where each individual's work would be identified to the group. For instance, this could involve a group event around checking for errors, so the whole group could see in real time if the code fails—and further, whose section of the code failed. Alternatively, engineers could check each other's code. These techniques also allowed Maria to stop wasting time as a solo micromanager by making the team police itself. After these changes were implemented, one engineer reported, "Everyone on the team dreaded being the one to have the code that wasn't ready or the code that failed."

That being said, the power of publicity need not involve public shaming.[35] Maria ultimately framed the public code-checking event as a celebration for meeting the deadline. But even in that less formal setting, everyone wanted to do well and look good in front of their peers. Maria used people's egos—their desire to be respected for their work—to turn them into better team players.[36]

We've seen how the Winner's Trap emerges when people aren't committed enough to team goals. Rather than moving toward a goal together, free riders take advantage of the system by claiming more for themselves and contributing less than they should to the group. We'll now see how the Winner's Trap leads people to overcommit to ideas that aren't working.

Game Over

Sometimes, managers remain fixated on failing ideas, and because they're used to being winners, they refuse to quit and accept the loss. They keep playing the game and investing resources in bad ideas, escalating their commitment to those ideas, and preventing resources from freely flowing to better ideas.

Remember Chris, the smooth-talking job candidate in chapter 2 who was hired based on his sparkling performance on the job interview—even though he wasn't equipped for the job? While the Expertise Trap got him hired, the Winner's

Trap took over once the evidence of his poor performance started mounting. Instead of cutting his losses and accepting the sunk costs, Chris's boss sent him for expensive trainings. The extra training couldn't address the root problem; namely, that Chris wasn't qualified to do the job. It was only after Chris lost his company a $3 million contract that his superiors admitted that they had made a mistake. As they dealt with that fallout and reduced his responsibilities, he grew annoyed at his subordinates and occasionally boiled over in angry rants. Several key players on the team found alternative opportunities, and the others who worked for him just waited (and hoped) he would get fired. After Chris was ultimately dismissed, one employee quantified the damage: "Chris received salary and benefits for two and a half years and multiple man-hours were wasted in either dealing with him, cleaning up his mess, or simply discussing him."

Chris occasionally seemed like he was improving, justifying their strategy of further investing in him. Most of all, though, it wasn't easy to come to terms with the fact that they hadn't picked a star. It was psychologically easier to spend time, money, and resources to keep moving forward in the hopes that they'd correct the issue, than to admit that they were wrong.

But here ants have another thing to teach us. Scientists have discovered that ants facing blocked paths respond differently from humans stuck in the Winner's Trap. To examine their approach, scientists created two "highways" leading to sugar syrup and created overcrowding on one of those highways. Instead of competing, the ants cooperated: Whenever one lane was jammed, the ants rapidly directed the others to the less crowded highway.[37] The gridlock cleared fluidly. The ants thus did two things that those in the Winner's Trap don't. First, they were generous: the ants on the fast road immediately signaled their fellow ants and shared their new newfound information. And second, the other ants quickly acknowledged their own mistakes. The ants on the blocked road wasted no time in moving over to the faster-moving lane. While they were patient with the slow movers who carried food, they weren't patiently rationalizing their own error by persisting on a blocked path. As small as ants are and as simple as their nervous systems may be, their decision rules allow them to see the big picture in a way that humans ensnared in the Winner's Trap often cannot.

Unlike ants, once people have committed to a course of action, they often become locked into it and don't want to back down.[38] Instead of making the hard call to accept the sunk costs, update their previous (wrong) knowledge, and relinquish the project as soon as evidence of failure starts to roll in, people often employ "quick fixes" that offer short-run relief but eventually cost the company significantly in terms of time and money.

To escape this variant of the Winner's Trap, the crucial skill lies in giving up, quitting, and being able to call "Game over!"—exactly what winners have been conditioned *not* to do. Highly effective leaders are, by disposition, persistent and optimistic—qualities that normally enable them to drive projects to successful completion. But these qualities also lead managers to feel that they have to defend a project to its finish, even if it is not meeting standards. What makes relinquishing a goal even harder is that people also know that their organizational lives depend on keeping their projects afloat. If one of their decisions is labeled a loser rather than a winner, they could get fired, miss out on a promotion, or lose a bonus.

Fortunately, there are ways to help yourself and your team members cut the losses and emerge as winners in the end, even while admitting failure. Let's consider three specific strategies that help train "winners" to be better "quitters"—that is, admit losses and extricate themselves from the occasional bad decision—rather than digging a deeper hole.

BRING IN FRESH EYES. Psychologist Barry Staw challenged people with a business investment decision that by any counts looked bad. The hitch was that money had already been invested. Should they quit funding it and accept a sure loss, or continue to invest? Staw found that the leaders who made the initial (bad) investment were the most likely to continue to throw good money away. The solution? Get external evaluation. It is precisely because product champions have a personal stake in the project that they cannot be objective. Thus, independent evaluators can check the champion at various stages.[39] Unlike the champion, the independent evaluator can see the bigger picture and doesn't feel trapped to escalate at each step. This independent evaluator does not have to be an expensive external consultant. That person could be a mutually agreed-upon apolitical voice within the firm, or even an anonymous group of evaluators who could gauge the project's potential without feeling pressured by the politics of the situation.

When organizational researchers Hirotaka Takeuchi and Ikujiro Nonaka observed companies including Toyota, Honda, and Fuji, they developed an iterative approach to product development, whereby software teams can adapt to constantly changing demands from stakeholders.[40] A critical part of their agile process involves *sprint reviews*, demoing the product at various critical stages to stakeholders, users, and other interested project managers who can test whether the project is meeting its targets at specific stages. While there are certainly times when a project needs to be insulated from criticism and given the time to incubate, open testing and review can help ensure the project's progress.

REWARD ACCURACY, NOT OPTIMISM. During sprint reviews, the key is to reward accuracy rather than optimism, self-delusional persistence, and risk taking.[41] This is accomplished by instituting clear protocols whereby people make predictions and keep track of them. One best practice is agreeing on the "DoD" (definition of done), which focuses people on clearly measurable milestones, as compared to assessments that can be biased by wishful thinking (e.g., "We're 65 percent of the way there."). Even if your team isn't designing software, these principles instill discipline because they push you to define what's measurable up front, and identify decision points at which the project could be terminated if the results don't meet expectations.

GIVE DEAD PROJECTS A FUNERAL. The idea of learning from failure is not a news flash to most managers. Yet, we still see companies celebrate successful projects, while quietly shelving "dead" projects, so that they live in corporate memory only as jokes or cautionary tales.

As one example, consider IBM's Stretch computer.[42] Stephen Dunwell, who championed the machine, optimistically promised a computer that would be a hundred times faster than existing machines. Its actual speed was only thirty times faster. When IBM president Thomas Watson Jr. saw the prototype, he immediately declared it to be a failure. Only nine of the machines were ever sold, the product's price was significantly discounted because of its failure to meet the promises made about it, and the company took a $20 million loss. Dunwell was demoted—and the champion became a loser. But, as decades passed, the lines demarcating failure and success blurred. Many of the engineering features of the Stretch appeared in IBM's most successful computers, including pre-fetch memory, memory protection, and program-controlled interruption that allowed for multi-tasking, hardware-based error-detection. Dunwell was later named a fellow—one of IBM's highest honors—for his contributions, and Watson graciously apologized for dismissing his accomplishments.

When identifying projects that need to be stopped, it's easy to focus on where things went wrong. But recognizing the effort's successes can help combat the Winner's Trap. To destigmatize failure, those who contributed to the project could assess what worked and what didn't, rather than writing it off as a blanket failure.

For example, senior leaders at Etsy suspected that teams and managers might fall into the Winner's Trap if the company commended only successful ideas. So Etsy instituted a "Best Failure of the Year" award. By establishing a "failure budget," the company sent the message to employees that failure is a natural part of experimentation that they could extract value from. Questions for learning might include: What were the challenges in this project? What would you have done differently, looking back on things? What content knowledge can you apply to future projects? What process knowledge can you apply to future projects? And are there other departments in the company that could find this information useful?

Even when projects succeed, critically evaluate them to seek out missed opportunities for improvement, near misses and lucky breaks that allowed them to avoid failure, and areas for process improvement. Researchers studying NASA employees documented the tendency to treat near-misses as successes rather than as failures—which caused them to miss crucial opportunities for learning.[43] These strategies allow leaders to loosen the definition of both *winner* and *loser*, and shift the team's focus to learning.

Conclusion

Winners are used to being the best and getting the most. Their competitive approach propels them to be creative and unique, and to rise to the top of various situations, but it also creates significant waste as people miss opportunities to learn and collaborate with others. We've described several situations that can trip the winner's competitive switch: the challenge of admitting someone else knows more; the temptation to give less and take more from teams; and the tendency to avoid accepting a loss on failing ideas. By bringing a competitive mindset to these situations, people create traffic jams at work where they compete for attention and resources instead of cooperating, and avoid the threatening situations that allow them to ultimately hone their competitive skills and improve performance.

We also considered strategies that allow managers to successfully unblock these jams. Sometimes teams become locked in competitive situations where a win for one is a loss for others. To get beyond zero-sum incentives, which focus people on both individual and financial goals, managers can put other resources in play that could enlarge the pie: through recognition and publicity, or internal opportunities. When people bring their competitive spirit inside the team, managers have to use the team as referees. This can channel people's innate tendencies to impress others into value creation rather than waste production. Finally, winners have to learn to be quitters (at the right times), and managers have to clearly call "Game over!" Admitting defeat isn't a sign of weakness but an opportunity to learn from the experience and translate that knowledge to a new innovative effort.

Escaping the Winner's Trap isn't about piously setting aside self-interest, but about channeling competitive instincts and managing the competitive terrain so that people play on widened paths with clearly marked boundaries. In chapter 4, we'll consider how people who tip too far in the other direction— that is, become overly concerned about others' interests—can also lose the signal.

CHAPTER 4

The Agreement Trap

In 2007, Rhode Island Hospital, Brown University's prestigious teaching hospital, performed three wrong-site brain surgeries—an alarmingly high "miss" rate. For two of these patients, the doctors cut through the wrong side of the skull, and in the third case, the doctor stopped after cutting through the patient's scalp. The mistakes fortunately did not kill or permanently injure the patients. However, there are plenty of stories of patients in other hospitals who haven't been so lucky. For instance, patients have had the wrong leg amputated, and a British man who was scheduled for a minor procedure received an accidental vasectomy.[1]

In medicine, such incidents are known as *never events*, because they should never occur. The signals may be loud, clear, and obvious. Yet people miss them, and they occur quite frequently. For example, wrong-site surgeries are estimated to occur about forty times a week across the United States. One-quarter of orthopedic surgeons are likely to make a wrong-site mistake at some point during their careers.[2]

Investigations into what went wrong at the Rhode Island Hospital revealed that the issues were due to the group dynamics in the operating room. In one of these incidents, the chief neurosurgery resident and the nurse had established the correct side of the skull ahead of time, but when the doctor marked and cut the wrong side, they did not speak up. In another case, the nurse did speak up, asking the doctor why he did not confirm the site of the surgery on the consent form. When the doctor said he knew the correct side, she asked him if he was sure. He replied that he was, and she did not push him further to follow the procedure or directly state that he was wrong. He then proceeded to cut into the wrong side.[3]

This type of self-censoring is not confined to the operating room. When people are communicating with a higher-ranking colleague in an organization, it's not uncommon for them to put their own points of view aside. But whether it's because they trust the other person's expertise over their own, want to keep the peace for the sake of the team, or just want to avoid embarrassment, these situations can cause more hurt than help. Additionally, the institution—the hospital in this case—can incur massive fines, malpractice lawsuits, and new reporting requirements in addition to loss of reputation. Rhode Island Hospital was fined $150,000 and required to install video cameras in its operating theaters.[4]

The Cost of Silence

In an organizational context, never events refer to situations that in hindsight are no-brainers. As such, they seem far removed from the wicked problems that challenge cognitive limits. The complexity of these situations doesn't lie in discovering a breakthrough solution but instead in having the courage to simply *articulate* it. People often remain silent and avoid sending vital signals because speaking up and taking action involves a social cost.[5]

For instance, managers may praise, retain, and even promote undeserving people rather than offer them clear negative feedback. Subordinates may fail to speak up when a superior is about to make a mistake. And staff may not bring an emergency situation to the attention of leadership. Thus, action without traction occurs because people aren't willing to get to the heart of the problem. The group ends up monitoring the noise rather than the signals, which may result in potentially catastrophic outcomes.

Unlike the patient who awakes to find that the wrong limb was removed, never events in the management world can often go undetected for months or years because the damage and loss may not be immediately obvious. For instance, in 2015, Volkswagen was caught outfitting its diesel engines with software that could cheat emissions testing. Observers were struck by the fact that no one had blown the whistle, since the development of these engines had begun ten years earlier.[6] The scheme was discovered only when a clean air group, ironically hoping to prove that diesel ran clean, actually tested the engines.[7]

However, just like a medical never event, managerial never events can result in tragic loss of life. General Motors' faulty ignition switches were linked to over three hundred deaths. A 325-page inquest report helped explain the absence of whistleblowers. A GM safety inspector told investigators that he feared voicing his concerns after seeing his predecessor "pushed out of the job for doing just that."[8] As a result, the company had to recall thirty million cars, and it paid $900 million to the US government to halt a criminal investigation into the incident.[9]

Whenever people with knowledge, information, and ideas self-censor and put their valid concerns aside for fear that they will antagonize their teammates and superiors or lose support and advancement in the company, they have fallen into the Agreement Trap. When in the Agreement Trap, they either fail to transmit the high-value signal or distort it.

To be sure, not everyone who raises a dissenting voice is correct, and certain self-appointed devil's advocates can derail essential consensus building. But if an organization does not invite, much less tolerate, controversial viewpoints, it is baiting the Agreement Trap. Escape from this trap does not simply lie in declaring that one is open to ideas. In fact, even though we've never heard any managers openly declare that they are against free speech and are looking to promote yes-men, their employees can have very different perceptions. Evidence from large surveys indicates that only 29 percent of first-level supervisors felt encouraged to express their opinions, and that 70 percent of employees felt afraid to express their opinions.[10] Why is there such a gap between what managers say and how their employees feel? It's easy to advocate free speech when you happen to agree with what's being said. But in practice, making space for those who disagree ends up being a much more complicated and uncomfortable process. Indeed, conflicts about what to do can quickly become conflicts about people, then undermine social relations and team performance.[11]

To understand and address these challenges, you have to look below the surface—beyond managers' espoused values about free speech—to the unspoken norms in groups and teams. These are the *psychological contracts* mentioned in chapter 3, the unspoken but binding, mutually agreed-upon norms of collegial behavior that operate when people at work relate to each other.[12]

More often than not, psychological contracts govern benign and kind forms of collegiality such as celebrating birthdays or doing favors for one another. Unlike managers caught in the Winner's Trap, those in the Agreement Trap aren't driven by getting a personal win for themselves. They are instead overly compassionate to others and empathic about their colleagues' issues.[13] They are team players who don't disrupt the group by raising controversial issues and concerns. They give credit to others and compromise in negotiations. They "take one for the team," because instigating a conflict would threaten the implicit psychological contract.

Occasionally, however, the psychological contract pressures managers to turn a blind eye to data or to self-censor in the face of potential conflict. When there are serious issues such as in the case of GM and Volkswagen, and they remain silent instead of signaling trouble to the group, the company heads straight for a garbage can decision or a never event. Organizational researchers identified five rationales that people use to explain to themselves why speaking up would be risky, inappropriate, and perhaps even unethical. These quotations from managers at one large corporation reveal these excuses that people use to justify their silence and maintain the psychological contract:[14]

- "People get so attached to their projects; their projects become part of their self-image and self-worth so it's not acceptable to question them." In other words, don't speak up because suggestions are personal criticisms, and therefore offensive.

- "There's that feeling, that belief, that you should go in [to forums where voice is possible] extremely prepared. That you should cover every area, not go out on a limb, don't reach or overextend any conclusions without substantiation." In other words, don't speak up unless you are 100 percent certain you are right.

- "My boss would see [speaking up to his boss] as undermining and insubordinate." In other words, don't speak up because that would bypass the established hierarchy.

- "Managers hate to be put on the spot in front of others. It is best to brief them first one-on-one so the boss doesn't look bad in front of the group." In other words, don't speak up in public or you'll embarrass people.

- "What good is it going to do me to stand up and have a legitimate question or maybe challenge them about something? Nothing but put me lower in the basement." Or "If I disagree, they would maybe hold a grudge against me—like at our end-of-year review, they might be nitpicky." In other words, don't speak up, as you'll risk retaliation.

Each justification causes organizations to squander a vault of critical signals in plain sight. But the problem with speaking up and sending the signal is that it's a pointless exercise in action without traction (and career suicide) if the organization doesn't have your back.

This chapter is about balancing teamwork and collegiality with the need to speak up and disagree in important situations—that is, ensuring that meaningful signals are communicated loud and clear—and indeed amplified—as you face off against problems. We introduce methods by which organizations, managers, and leaders can confront others and extricate themselves and their people from the Agreement Trap and its costs.

Let's consider some of the most common situations in which the Agreement Trap emerges. As difficult as it is to challenge a boss, people also find themselves in the Agreement Trap with subordinates, offering "soft" feedback that elicits no results. It is easier to offer praise than to initiate a pointed discussion of shortcomings, and managers certainly are more likely to give "harsher" (more truthful, uncensored) feedback when recording their comments compared with giving the same feedback in person.[15] Just as people tiptoe around issues of diversity, they also struggle to communicate with their closest associates—the very people who should make them feel most comfortable. We conclude by describing some best practices that allow people to engage in productive conflict. Specifically, we discuss ways to have direct, courageous, and strategic negotiations—and even initiate conflicts—about task issues, while mitigating the interpersonal, unproductive aspects of conflict.[16]

The Fragile Ego Illusion

Alexis is a thirty-five-year-old, single attorney in San Francisco. She often finds that her business card is a conversation stopper. She notes wryly: "I've been told by well-meaning relatives: 'Don't talk about work on a date, dumb it down, and it's bad to earn so much money because guys will be scared of you.' And I got the word 'intimidating' a lot."[17] Alexis falls into a category known as SWANS—strong women achievers, no spouse. Most SWANS surveyed believe their career and educational success lessens their chances of getting married. To avoid this "success penalty," many play dumb so that they are less likely to threaten others.[18]

However, SWANS are not the only ones who dumb themselves down because they fear that they might intimidate others. For example, men and women who went to an Ivy League school sometimes say, "I went to school in Boston," when asked where they went to college. They don't want to drop the H-bomb, or reveal that they went to Harvard, which would, they presume, threaten others.[19] So they try to disguise that fact, sometimes in a geographical game of twenty questions, assuming that this longer and more convoluted conversation is the humane approach.

The *fragile ego illusion* is the belief that others will be offended or upset if they find out how great we are and how much we have accomplished and so, we spare them the embarrassment and self-loathing by minimizing our accomplishments and taking a back seat.[20] The fragile ego illusion is one manifestation of the Agreement Trap—people turn the volume down because they want others in their social networks to like them, and so they act in ways to make themselves less intimidating.

This sounds harmless and considerate for the most part—but the problem is that we are not the only ones trying to shield others from our "greatness." Others are treating us in much the same way, and the result is a form of organizational pluralistic ignorance: no one really knows what anyone thinks because all the signals are lost in the noise. People caught in the Agreement Trap are so excessively anxious about straining relations with others that they put aside their own interests and may avoid critical business issues.[21]

As with the "Where did you go to college?" question, people engage in unnecessarily convoluted conversations where they rarely disagree with others or fail to state their positions directly. In our observations of business meetings, we have often noticed conversations where people would not openly object to ideas, but kill them with faint praise ("Yes, John, that's really great . . . " "Cindy, you really made a nice insight there . . . "). The ideas would then be quietly tossed into the garbage can without explanation. In tiptoeing around people's feelings, the Agreement Trap causes people to engage in convoluted conversations and indirect communications that only someone with a PhD in linguistics could translate, wasting everyone's time in the process.

The Fragile Ego Double Standard

In our research, we uncovered a double standard when it comes to ego resilience. Specifically, while people often describe another person's ego as delicate, they refer to their own egos as if they were made of steel (e.g., "I'm so thick-skinned, I love criticism," "I grow with every failure," "I always surround myself with people who are smarter than me"). When we surveyed MBA students working in project groups, we observed the same pattern— people assumed that others felt 46 percent more intimidated by their talents than they reported feeling intimidated by others. They were 48 percent more likely to minimize their strengths when dealing with someone who they thought perceived them as a threat, and the more they inferred that they threaten the other person, the more they minimized their strengths.[22]

We explored managers' fears that others felt intimidated, and perhaps envious, simply by their very presence. This phenomenon was surfaced in our classes, in which our students often described having to deal with bosses who felt threatened by them at work. One newly minted MBA confessed that, because she was the youngest person on her team and also the leader, that others were resentful and she felt trapped. However, when we questioned the senior people on her team, they said they were not at all intimidated and did not regard her age to be an issue. Our research on envy and threat, described in chapter 3, indicates that these feelings are often very real. But what if, we wondered, these pernicious beliefs were merely a figment of the imagination?

We embarked on a research program to study this question. In one study, we placed students in the role of either boss or employee in a challenging conversation. We hinted to some participants that the boss might feel threatened by their skills and abilities when, in fact, the boss actually had no information about their skills. The employees who assumed that their own talents would be threatening elicited less favorable reactions from the boss. Even though people rarely communicate these perceptions about threat to one another explicitly (e.g., "I understand you feel intimidated by my intelligence and beauty"), interaction partners clearly sense them. The more threatened people assume that others are, the less others enjoy interacting with them. Even when people play down their talents, people still perceive them as self-promoting—given the condescending assumptions that underlie their actions ("I know it's hard for you to deal with my high intelligence, so I'll turn it down so as not to offend you"). They weren't hated because they were smart, or beautiful, or because they went to an Ivy League school, but rather because they were patronizing instead of just being direct and forthright.

Let's consider three more specific places where the Agreement Trap emerges, leading to weak and distorted signals rather than clear communication: communications with subordinates, people of different ethnicities, and close relationships.

Weak and Distorted Feedback to Subordinates

It's certainly hard to contradict the boss. But dealing with an underperforming subordinate should be far easier, right? Well, consider a story that one executive shared that seemed to us nearly impossible to believe at first. Laura was a competent administrative assistant in many areas, but was failing miserably at what is arguably an administrative assistant's major responsibility: answering phones. She would sit at her desk and just let the phone ring. It was inexplicable behavior. While her managers looked the other way initially, figuring the problem would correct itself, their next step was to use oblique methods to give her feedback, such as "general" e-mails sent to the whole admin pool—though obviously directed at her. Not surprisingly, these e-mails had little effect. Over the course of three weeks, no one bothered to communicate with her directly.

On the surface, this minor behavioral problem appears to exact only negligible costs. But even a trivial conflict such as this one can quickly cost the organization hundreds of thousands of dollars between the inefficiency in not getting messages, potential lost business, wasted time, and demoralized staff. If poor performers are not given feedback, their behavior becomes an acceptable social norm and a persistent spending trap.

When one manager finally confronted Laura directly, the "why" behind her behavior was quickly revealed: it turned out she was a germophobe and at some point had determined that the phone was dirty. As a result of this single, direct conversation, the manager changed her phone to a hands-free headset and fixed the problem.

As unbelievable as this story may seem, it's just one of the many never events executives have shared with us about individuals in their workplace who've been praised instead of given feedback and are retained and even promoted when they've failed to meet performance expectations. It's often justified as "nice," but it's neither nice nor fair from the point of view of the high performers who pick up the slack and essentially finance the incompetents.

Tiptoeing around Diversity

The Agreement Trap often emerges with respect to diversity. Indeed, diversity has become such a sensitive topic that it may be risky to even ask questions about it. Consider Randall, a human resources manager, who asked for data on whether the large investment of time and money his company was spending on a new diversity program actually led to improvements. "I was simply trying to understand what we were getting out of this spending," he said, "but it got touchy. I think that some people felt I was anti-diversity, or maybe worse." Many managers are not sure what is or is not appropriate, so they avoid the conversation altogether. As a result, the tangible benefits of these efforts and training programs often go unmeasured.[23]

How can people get more comfortable with having direct conversations, even with respect to touchy issues like race and gender? Researcher Evan Apfelbaum observed the evasion about race firsthand when he had African American and white students interact via an "I spy" game where the task was to identify faces. White subjects were paired with African American counterparts (who were in on the study) to examine how the white participants managed the topic of race in conversation. In the experiment, white students were shown twenty pictures of faces, while their partner picked a "target" photo. The white partner's job was to identify who the target person was by asking the fewest questions possible. The faces varied by gender, race, hairstyle, facial expression, and so forth. Even though the white test participants could ask any question to quickly narrow down the possibilities, most avoided asking questions about race, even though it would have led to a quick discovery. People walked on eggshells asking a series of questions that avoided the topic of race because they were petrified about being perceived as racist or offending the other person. The result of the "colorblind" communication was that the interview was stilted, awkward, and unproductive, and the African American students on the receiving end regarded it as annoying and even condescending. Conversely, when the white person simply asked, "Is the person African American?" instead of operating as if race was a taboo topic or liability, tensions eased, the problem was solved, and conversations were much more relaxed.[24] The people involved actually liked, respected, and connected with one another.

To get comfortable with having these potentially sensitive discussions, a key technique is to turn the *implicit* social contract—i.e., people's assumptions about what they should do as "good group members" and what they expect from others—into an *explicit* one. To eliminate ambiguity about what people expect from each other, talk about the group process before the work of the group commences, so members can clarify their goals and the best way to work together. In chapter 6, we'll talk more about how to create this connective tissue between group members, but this discussion is especially important in situations where people are diverse and therefore likely to have different assumptions about how to work together.

Second, rather than sidestepping issues and playing "colorblind," build a history of fair and respectful actions to pave the ground for more challenging conversations.[25] With investments in trust building, a poorly worded message is less likely to be automatically interpreted as "racist" and given the benefit of the doubt, and more likely to be openly addressed. For example, instead of "buying" their diversity credentials with expensive networking events and training programs that aren't always effective, C-suite executives at one company carved out time during their business trips to meet and have a meal with diverse potential hires at colleges across the country. Even though the company was located in a remote area that lacked diversity, this more subtle (and inexpensive) gesture acknowledged their diverse customers and employees, and communicated their willingness to learn from them.

The Agreement Trap in Close Relationships

It's unsurprising that people may tread carefully in manager-subordinate communication, or when they're working with people of different races and genders. And so it would seem that the Agreement Trap would be avoided when negotiating with those we're close to, whether it's a friend, coworker, or colleague. But the Agreement Trap can be especially wasteful in the very closest of relationships because people avoid conflict to keep the peace. And they often justify the waste as a "gift," "self-sacrifice," or "taking one for the team."

A perfect example of such a lose-lose outcome between close friends due to the Agreement Trap is found in O. Henry's story "The Gift of the Magi."[26] In the story, a husband and wife each sacrifice their most treasured possession to buy a gift they think the other will enjoy. Of course, they don't discuss it in advance; the wife cuts her beautiful hair to buy a chain for the man's treasured watch, while the husband sells his watch to buy his wife an expensive comb for her hair. In the process, they both lose: the wife no longer needs the comb and the husband no longer needs the watch chain. Reading the story as wistful romantics, one might think, "Look how well they know each other! Look what they give up for that love!" Yet through the lens of waste, this story is about the couple's faulty communication. If only they had signaled their needs and wants, they could have reached a win-win agreement instead of making sacrifices that catapulted them into a lose-lose agreement.

Inefficiencies like this can emerge precisely because people are in a close relationship. In fact, one study found that dating couples negotiated *worse* deals than strangers. They did not want to relentlessly search for an optimal agreement, so they satisficed and settled for the lowest-hanging fruit—a "good enough" option that both could reluctantly agree on, even if it made neither very happy.[27] Squandering value in negotiations is simply easier than disturbing the relationship. And while people who have a relational approach to negotiation create inefficient economic outcomes, they do feel satisfied with the relationship.[28] But after spinning a poor deal as "taking one for the team," they often realize later that they could have created a much more satisfying outcome if they felt more comfortable pushing the other person a bit more.

Checking assumptions in this context is especially important because people who are close to each other—longstanding friends, spouses, and teammates—are prone to speak to each other indirectly. A Chinese proverb describes the careful ways people should communicate negative information in close relationships, warning, "Do not remove a fly from your friend's forehead with a hatchet." The problem is that indirect speech can lead to signal distortion. In the example below, in which a woman is trying to communicate a command to her husband, each sentence represents a range of things she could say. Each is progressively less direct and, consequently, requires a great deal more mental processing by the receiver:[29]

1. Close the door.

2. Can you close the door?

3. Would you close the door?

4. It might help to close the door.

5. Would you mind awfully if I asked you to close the door?

6. Did you forget the door?

7. How about a little less breeze?

8. I really don't want the cats to get out of the house.

The more indirect the delivery, the more likely the husband is—if he is not on high alert—to miss the ultimate meta-message. The result is a needless argument. And here's an organizational example where increasingly indirect feedback distorts the signal, garbling a criticism into a compliment:

1. You've underperformed on this project.

2. Your contributions have failed to meet our expectations on this project.

3. It would help to know why you're having a hard time contributing to this project.

4. Can you share what you've found challenging on this project?

5. I'd like to understand your point of view about this project.

6. Your input on this project would be very valuable.

If ambiguous messages are directed to someone who doesn't grasp them, signal distortion occurs. The wife thinks she's clear when she's talking about the cats, but she's done a conversational dance which forces the husband to make seven more inferential leaps than if she'd just asked him to close the door!

Escaping the Agreement Trap is about getting comfortable probing what it is people actually want and know without making assumptions and losing value in interpersonal conflict.

Consider the following specific behaviors to escape the Agreement Trap.

Find Your Inner Negotiator

Most people find negotiations stressful and uncomfortable. In fact, the very word negotiation can be a conversation-stopper. Many managers don't even use the word, rather they say that they are "working things out." Negotiation, which is often associated with being pushy, aggressive, and demanding, is often not part of people's implicit social contract with their colleagues.[30] However, we've found a way to help people get more comfortable with these conversations and rethink their implicit assumptions. We tell them that anytime they cannot get what they want without the cooperation of others, they are negotiating. Soon, they begin to realize that they are negotiating all the time.

There are two main categories of negotiations. *Scripted* negotiations include such activities as buying a car or negotiating with a new hire about salary. The majority of negotiations, however, are *unscripted*, such as figuring out who is going to pick up the kids, who is cooking dinner, or, at the office, who is meeting the client. Each of these covert negotiations reveals a moment where people in the Winner's Trap claim value for themselves and those in the Agreement Trap tend to pass it up. The point is not to turn every interaction into a painful haggling process—but instead to reframe taken-for-granted-assumptions about the social contract so that people can pursue value-creating conversations.

Get Beyond "Nice"

Some people fall into the Agreement Trap because they're typecast as "nice"; for others, it's the expectations that come with their gender. For women in particular, "niceness" creates Agreement Traps in the workplace. Studies have found that as environments become more competitive, men's performance improves, but women's does not.[31] And, whereas men received a "disagreeable dividend," i.e., their salaries were higher the less cooperative, gentle, and compliant they were, this characteristic paid off far less for women.[32] That's because women expect (and receive) backlash when they appear aggressive and competitive.[33] Women pressed into "nice" strategies may waste thousands of dollars of both value that could have benefited organizations, and promotions and bonuses that they should earn for themselves.

Gender aside, the reason why capitulating and conceding in each of these interactions doesn't help relationships is because you are in long-term relationships with people who have short-term memories. This means that the concession you offer today may be appreciated for the moment, but people quickly forget the favors they owe—while displaying excellent memory of the favors they're owed.[34]

But there are ways to escape these patterns of capitulation:

CHALLENGE YOUR OWN STEREOTYPE. Rather than seeing the stereotype as baggage that holds you back, use it to inspire yourself to fight back against it. Leigh and researchers Laura Kray and Adam Galinsky conducted an investigation to show how this works.[35] They reminded some women of the docile female stereotype immediately before a mixed-gender negotiation; others were not reminded of the stereotype. The result? The women who had consciously thought of the stereotype reacted against it and negotiated harder, as if to say, "I'm not that type of pushover woman." This suggests that if women—or others who are considered too "nice"—want to avoid the Agreement Trap, they should acknowledge their own negative stereotypes, and then take active steps to prove them wrong. If you are a man who's been pigeonholed into the "nice" box, simply remind yourself of being labeled a "cream puff" to inspire yourself to prove it wrong!

MAKE "NICE" WORK IN YOUR FAVOR. Regardless of whether you're a man or woman, you can also leverage the "nice" stereotype. For women, this is the *protective mother figure*.[36] When female negotiators imagined they were negotiating on behalf of their teams (as a "mama bear" of sorts), they were as successful as were men. Men who feel uncomfortable asking for resources for themselves can employ this strategy too. They can simply frame their request as a means to benefit their team ("I do need to push harder here, because if my team doesn't get these resources, we won't be able to excel on this project") or the people they are serving ("I understand that this is a big ask, but without it, we won't be able to deliver on the customer's expectations here"). For people normally straitjacketed into "nice" identities, negotiating for the group allows them to find their inner hardball negotiator.

Be Strategic, Not Soft

When it comes to negotiating, most people think they have to choose between being either tough as nails or a cream puff. By choosing between tough or soft approaches, they miss the win-win alternative: be a *strategic negotiator*—hard on the problem but respectful of the people.[37]

How can you think like a strategic negotiator? Even though empathy is supposedly a good thing in managing conflict, negotiators who empathize with the other party are actually less effective than those who simply take the perspective of the other party.[38] Empathy is imagining how it would feel to inhabit the role of your negotiation partner. Perspective-taking, in contrast, is simply recognizing the other party's interests.

Author Gloria Steinem tells an anecdote she calls "ask the turtle," which illustrates the difference. As a geology student doing fieldwork, she discovered a giant turtle that had crawled out of the river and seemed to be struggling in a muddy embankment on the roadside. She tugged and pushed at the angrily snapping turtle and finally returned it to the river. At that moment, her professor observed, "You know, that turtle probably spent a month crawling up that dirt road to lay its eggs in the mud by the side of the road, and you just put it back in the river." In spite of her empathy for the turtle, she failed to understand its instinctive motivation.[39]

Indeed, negotiators who are told to imagine what the other side is *thinking* achieve more successful outcomes than those who are told to imagine what the other side is *feeling*. When people empathize with their adversaries, they are concerned for them and take on all their emotional baggage. But by thinking through the adversary's position and point of view, people become more strategic, rather than operating on uninformed assumptions.

In her research on negotiation, Leigh devised three strategies that help negotiators "ask the turtle"—so that they can avoid such assumptions and negotiate maximum value even when negotiating within close relationships:[40]

- Determine your priorities: Simply asking, "What are my most important issues?" before a negotiation can prepare you to take full advantage of the value up for grabs. This question jump-starts your ability to think like a trader. Once you identify what's most important, you can think about what's less important and be ready to give that up to get what you really care about.

- Show (part of) your hand: Selectively signaling your most important issues to the other side can help you avoid making wasteful assumptions. By communicating with strategic honesty, the other party learns how to transact with you. And they have an opening to share their preferences as well.

- Play multiple choice: Devise multiple "package" deals that are essentially of equal value to you. Present three or more of these deals to your counterparts and ask them to choose. If they reject everything, simply ask which package is the *least* offensive. Their response will indicate what they value. This strategy is a powerful tool for negotiating with friends in particular. By making multiple offers of equivalent value simultaneously and letting the friend choose what's best, you can exchange clear, undistorted signals without making assumptions and needless concessions.[41]

Regardless of whether you are involved in a contentious negotiation with a supplier, or a seemingly dispassionate discussion with teammates who you've known well for years, these questions encourage the other party to signal their own interests. Indeed, in our investigations, people who openly revealed their own interests improved their own outcomes by 10 percent.[42]

Master the Art of Feedback

Now consider a situation where, rather than negotiating, you're giving an employee feedback. Managers know that the moment they begin to give critical feedback, employees often become defensive, looking to rationalize the criticism away as irrelevant or unfair (e.g., "He's criticizing me because he's threatened by my talent" or "Of course, you're unhappy with my work because you're biased"). Such responses prevent them from internalizing important feedback, and cause managers to dread—and even avoid—the process of giving feedback.

Control the "Why" in Feedback

One technique for preempting this defensiveness is to explain up front and clearly why the employee is getting the feedback rather than allowing the employee to derail your message by controlling the why. Try an honest preface the next time negative feedback is warranted, something like, "Laura, this is hard for me to say, and it would be easier for me to ignore the fact that this phone has been ringing and you're not responding to it. But the reason I want to talk to you is because I care about you and I want to see you succeed." Then deliver the critical comment. By letting the employee know the key (and developmental) reason they're getting that feedback (it serves their interests), it helps that feedback get past their armor of defensiveness. It's not a personal attack they've got to fend off—you're there to help them do better.

One reason why protocols can be so effective is because they control the "why." A nurse following a protocol is not checking to question the doctor's incompetence, but checking because that is the normal procedure.

But protocols are effective only if they are followed. Protocols that have been in place for years may fail to mitigate counter-productive incidents because people don't like following protocols and assume that they are careful enough without them. And it may still be hard for employees to share their feedback when they're speaking to someone higher up the hierarchy. Beyond creating safety cultures with no exceptions (e.g., consistent monitoring, and suspension for failing to follow protocols), other interventions have helped "level the authority gradient," allowing people who would typically lack status in that environment to feel more comfortable questioning decisions and challenging each other.[43] For instance, St. Francis Medical Center in Hartford, Connecticut recently implemented a policy whereby doctors, nurses, and technicians refer to each other by first name.[44] As another example, the Mayo Clinic instituted a "plus one" rule, meaning that any nurse can bring in another person to initiate a tough conversation, such as challenging a high-ranking doctor.[45] These interventions helped to create environments where people would be more comfortable to speak up and stop never events in their tracks.

Send the Signal and Make It Clear

In addition to avoiding giving feedback entirely, we've too often heard managers dilute their negative messages by cushioning them within the so-called "compliment sandwich" (compliment to soften the message, then criticize, then compliment again). Unfortunately, this rarely overcomes the employee's defensiveness: the compliments seem phony, and the negative feedback can be drowned out to the point of ineffectiveness. In order to make sure your message is getting across, throw away the sandwich and instead feed the "vegetables" first, and the "dessert" later. Psychologist Robert Cialdini prescribes using the negative message to grab attention, and then the positive message to shape the solution.[46] Consider two versions of the same messages:

> Laura, you've been one of the most careful members of the team for many years, and we'd like to keep it that way. But it's come to our attention that you've not been answering the phones. We need to talk, because you're at risk of losing your job.

> Laura, we need to talk, because you're at risk of losing your job. It's come to our attention that you've not been answering the phones. You've been one of the most careful members of our team for many years, and we'd like to keep it that way. Let's discuss how to fix this.

Delivering the first message is much easier. The positive language is front and center, it's far nicer, and you imagine (and hope) that the listener will get the point. But she actually might not. Your "nice" message waters down the seriousness of the situation. Research on the negativity bias indicates that negative information commands far more attention than positive information, and offers an attention-grabbing wake-up call.[47]

The problem with the negative message alone, however, is that while it grabs attention, it doesn't shape behavior. If you tell a child what not to do (e.g., "don't eat junk food"), you've not clearly told them what they should be doing (e.g., "eat your carrots and your spinach"). That's where positive action steps come in. In Laura's case, after the shock of the negative message, you can turn the message positive by articulating the specific actions steps ("Answering the phones is one of your major job responsibilities and if you're not able to meet them, you're at risk of losing your credibility and your job. Let's discuss some steps so you can get back on track in terms of meeting your job responsibilities.").

Join the Debate Team

The strategies above are about getting comfortable with direct conversation and surfacing disagreement. But let's take them one step further. Beyond getting past the fear of conflict, try to *purposefully encourage* conflict.

Researcher Kathy Phillips observes that diversity makes people smarter in the same way that exercise makes people stronger. Here is how it works: Truly diverse groups experience more painful interactions—that is, "discomfort, rougher interactions, a lack of trust, greater perceived interpersonal conflict, lower communication, less cohesion, more concern about disrespect, and other problems."[48] Phillips has reviewed decades of research finding that corporations with greater racial and gender diversity show higher performance. And, Tanya's research on international joint ventures in China with researchers Pamela Koch, Bradley Koch, and Oded Shenkar indicated that various types of cultural diversity in leadership style could create potential synergies, particularly when they didn't disrupt people's most rigidly held cultural assumptions.[49] This is because the pain can translate into intellectual gains when weaker ideas are challenged, contradictions lead to creative insight, and better insights emerge. For instance, Phillips finds that people may not even recognize an idea as different if it comes from someone who's socially (demographically) similar, yet they will pay attention to it and understand its uniqueness if it comes from someone who's socially (demographically) different. And she finds that people on diverse teams anticipate getting challenged more—causing them to prepare stronger arguments in response.

Actively structure your teams to create diverse perspectives. To put these principles into action, the video game production company Electronic Arts creates two teams when designing a new product—the budget team and the creative team—in order to elicit constructive, productive conflict. This tension becomes an engine that drives the company to produce the best product. According to former CEO John Riccitiello, "The smiley-face approach to management doesn't work in entertainment. Some people hope and dream and pray that spending more money and time will work. We double down on things that work, we tend to stop things that don't work."[50]

By purposefully creating these debates, you can help your team work through the pain of task conflicts and get the mental workout necessary to break out of the Agreement Trap. And by doing so on a regular basis, you encourage your people to engage in better, higher-value work that eliminates the cost of silence.

Conclusion

If you're stuck in an Agreement Trap, the challenge isn't about uncovering solutions. Instead, it is whether anyone is willing to speak up, act, and access the vault of knowledge.

To rationalize this inaction, the Agreement Trap creates an entire vocabulary to justify "nice" behavior. It's "colorblindness" when it's avoiding racial issues, "taking one for the team" when it's giving up value in negotiation between teammates, or softening tough feedback to avoid potential defensiveness. While your work environment may seem peaceful on the surface, these behaviors can cause underlying feelings of frustration, wasted time, and costly mistakes.

When managers embrace rather than avoid conflict and speak up rather than quiet down, they empower others to do the same. The conversations that result from debate-without-judgment allow organizations to directly address issues instead tap dancing around them. Moreover, the more managers and their teams practice this style of conversation, the better they become at focusing on the signal instead of the noise. In the next two chapters, we'll consider more detailed ways to design these team interactions so that you can extract the high value signals from the people and groups around you.

CHAPTER 5

The Communication Trap

The female frog faces a serious decision-making problem when it's time to mate. How can she locate the best mate amid the chorus of hundreds of croaking males in her pond? In many frog species, the "best" is the frog with the lowest-frequency croak, which indicates that he has a higher body mass.[1]

As the female frog participates in this deafening cocktail party, she's overwhelmed by the overcommunication. Her nervous system allows her to detect only those frogs in the small radius around her with croaks that meet a particular frequency, and the other frogs' communications will recede into the background as noise.[2] This means her options are in fact an illusion—she can only discern two or three frogs in her immediate area at a time. And, what's worse, as the volume exceeds certain levels, she no longer chooses the desirable, lower-frequency croaker. Trapped in the noise, she's transformed from an optimizer to a satisficer—who will make do with any mate.

Managers often are inundated with relentless organizational chatter, facing an environment much like the chaotic frog pond. That's the Communication Trap: managers find themselves within—and sometimes create—what organizational researchers call a "garbage can" decision making environment in which it becomes ever more difficult to distinguish the signal from the noise.[3] As managers face wicked problems, they search for more information to solve them. This is normally a strength, but it can also lead straight to action without traction when people become overloaded with information, decreasing the signal-to-noise ratio, and making the problem-solving environment even more complex and intractable.

According to signal-detection theory, people become fatigued when attempting to find a signal amid noise. Sometimes, people perceive a signal when there is none—as in *phantom text syndrome*, when they imagine that their phone has pinged them, but it actually hasn't; when they read an incredible internet story, then learn it's been retracted a few days later; or when they get an e-mail marked "urgent" that is in fact trivial. In signal-detection terms, these are all *false alarms*. Other times, people fail to realize that someone has sent them an important e-mail or text because it got lost in junk mail—a *miss* in signal-detection terms.[4]

Because overcommunication increases the noise, obscures high-value signals, and overloads human decision-making capacity, the temptation is then to invest in other technologies that help collect, sort, and analyze the information. A study done by McKinsey Global Institute reported that "interaction" workers (i.e., managers and professionals required to do significant interpersonal work and innovation, going beyond routine activity) spent approximately 19 percent of their work days gathering information (including searching their own e-mails) and another 28 percent of their time writing and responding to e-mails, which exceeded the 14 percent of time they spent actually collaborating with their colleagues.[5]

Given that the use of information technology will only increase, how can managers climb out of the Communication Trap and establish practices and behaviors that increase the signal-to-noise ratio at work? One often-mentioned antidote to communication technologies is to simply increase face-to-face time: more meetings, informal gatherings, office parties, and networking events.[6] But here's the catch: surveys indicate that people don't consider technology their number-one distraction at work; rather, it is *coworkers* who are more distracting![7] While technology has increased the speed and rate of communication, in many ways, it simply amplifies communication that already exists. You might find yourself in the Communication Trap if you're in a corporate culture that overloads you with face-to-face meetings as well.

The solution to the Communication Trap lies in thinking of communication as one of your most important, but undervalued and unregulated, resources. That is, while there are budgets to control your spending, there are no constraints on communication— you can generally talk to whomever you want, whenever you want, how often you want. So, people overproduce communications in some areas (contributing to the noise) and underproduce in others (missing out on high-value signals). Escaping the Communication Trap involves both recognizing how your own natural patterns of communication conspire to surround you in noise and finding ways to amplify high-value signals.

Consider the two types of noise that arise from this communication chorus, each of which involves significant opportunities for action without traction. The first is *redundant noise*, in which people lose high-value signals by communicating with people nearby or those with similar perspectives and expertise. Like the frog in the pond, managers at work often end up overcommunicating with those who are close by and similar to them, and filtering out contrasting opinions and information.[8] Every e-mail, meeting, or conversation with a like-minded colleague takes time and increases the noise without adding any novel, high-value signals.[9]

In this chapter, we introduce techniques that effectively streamline communication processes. We examine how changing footpaths at work can stimulate ideas and opportunities. And our own research indicates that this is about more than walking further: it's also about thinking more broadly about who you can learn from and challenging silo thinking by initiating interactions that otherwise might not occur.[10] When people communicate in cliques, they're investing time and resources to hear what they already may know. By expanding whom they talk to, that same investment in communication yields a higher rate of novel signals.[11]

Second, we consider *chaotic* noise emanating from hyper-communication in meetings, networking, and conversations that interferes with focusing on actual work.[12] It also involves the continuous search for information that doesn't necessarily help—and can actually reduce—your problem-solving ability. We'll present strategies to decrease both redundant and chaotic noise, which can help establish communication discipline, end the interminable search for information, and refocus your attention on the problems at hand.

Stop Bonding, Start Bridging

Take a look at the sociogram in figure 5-1. A sociogram is a way to capture and quantify social relationships. Each line represents a friendship link between people. As you look at these two distinctive clusters, and the chasm between them, can you guess where this network data came from?[13]

The network represents the friendship choices of fourth-graders studied by psychiatrist Jacob Moreno in 1934.[14] The cluster on the left is all boys, and the cluster on the right is all girls. If you remember fourth grade, you're probably not surprised by this nearly complete segregation of the sexes.

FIGURE 5-1

Moreno's sociogram

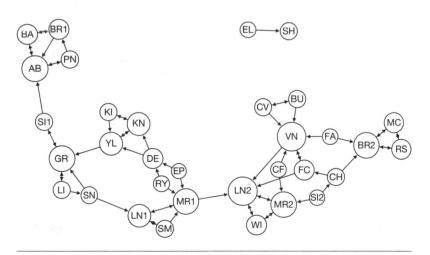

Now take a look at another very similar pattern of network ties in figure 5-2. These aren't fourth-graders, however. The squares represent Republicans, and the circles represent Democrats in the US Senate. Each tie represents a pair with a correlation of .33 or greater in their cosponsorship of bills—

FIGURE 5-2

Cosponsorship networks in the US Senate

Data: complete cosponsorship information for all S. and S. J. Res. Bills as of 3/1/2009. Tie exists between a pair of senators if the correlation of their cosponsorship profiles across all bills is 0.33 or greater. Senators who do not have correlation of cosponsorship of 0.33 or greater with any other senator are not included in the sociogram.

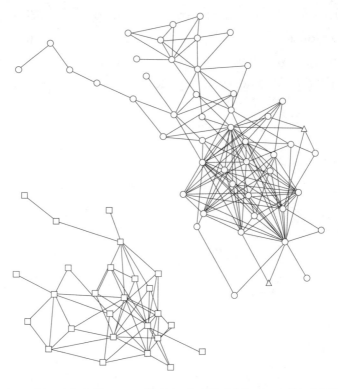

Source: Adapted from J. Cook, "Cosponsorship Networks in the U.S. Senate as of March 1, 2009," *Irregular Times*, http://irregulartimes.com/2009/03/01/cosponsorship-networks-in-the-us-senate-as-of-march-1-2009.

an indicator of their behavioral similarity.[15] In both networks, the sociogram visualizes a chasm between certain types of people and groups. Sociologist Ron Burt refers to these gaps in organizations where particular individuals and organizations are not communicating with each other as *structural holes* in the network.

Sandeep's technical and marketing teams were also divided by a structural hole, and faced a *silo mentality*—an excessive preoccupation and concern with their own group, function, and area, to the exclusion of others. When you think about your own workplace, can you identify places where similar patterns of cliquishness emerge? Where are there gaps in the communication network where people rarely reach across the aisle to move forward?

Managers often find themselves frustrated when they try to encourage their formal teams to build bridging ties and exchange information across silos. In spite of all of the communication technologies available, sociologist Robert Putnam observes that such gaps are on the rise in society. In his book *Bowling Alone*, he notices what might at first appear to be a trivial historical trend: while more people than ever are bowling, bowling *leagues* are in decline. People were either bowling alone or with friends. As he explored the pattern beyond bowling leagues, Putnam grew particularly interested in the importance of *bridging ties* versus *bonding ties*. Bonding ties involve homogeneous people (e.g., ties within an ethnic or religious group); bridging ties (e.g., bowling leagues, or ties between boys and girls, Republicans and Democrats) involve more heterogeneity by connecting diverse persons together.

Silos certainly perform a crucial function, allowing organizations to efficiently pattern and organize complexity. Consider how even the most mundane example—calling a company and getting passed around from department to department—reveals how complex problem solving gets categorized, sorted, and routed to different organizational silos.[16] But the neatly organized boundaries of these silos can also become liabilities when customers, clients, and stakeholders get bumped around from department to department and are looking for managers to integrate their skills and offer seamless solutions. Silos may simplify roles and encourage specialization, but they also create profound silences in the spaces between—spaces where people should be talking to each other.[17]

Inside these silos, people frequently miss high-value signals. Specifically, when people communicate solely within their groups, even though they may be hearing and producing a lot of sound, they are oversampling on the same perspectives. These silos are essentially echo chambers that reverberate with the noisy chatter of like-minded people.[18] Echo chambers are fine if friendship is the goal, but highly inefficient if people are searching for novel opportunities, innovations, and creative solutions. Familiar friends are comforting, but admittedly monotonous, and so people in echo chambers find themselves wasting time and energy in repetitious action, focusing on the same thing, time and time again, with no new ideas or improvement. And worse, the information inside an echo chamber tends to become more extreme and corrupted because it confirms people's preexisting ideas.

When people wander outside of their silos, they fill *structural holes*.[19] Some of what they hear may certainly be irrelevant and chaotic noise. But, in the process, they escape the redundant noise by exposing themselves to new and different ideas that check their misconceptions, and discovering unique opportunities to bring those ideas to life.[20] Let's consider some strategies to escape the habit of redundant communication inside the silo and locate novel signals.

Change Your Footpath at Work

Think about the most important conversation or interaction you had in the past month—an exchange that led to a valuable insight, opportunity, or creative possibility. Which communication medium was involved: Facebook? LinkedIn? Skype? A conference call? A face-to-face official meeting? When we've posed this question to executives, they rarely mention technology-enabled communications. And, almost without exception, they do not mention formal meetings, committees, or task forces either. Instead, we've discovered that their key breakthroughs most likely result from chance meetings: during cigarette breaks, coffee breaks, and even bathroom breaks! In fact, even nonsmokers tell us that they go on "smoke breaks" because the smokers "know everything." Some smokers even claim that they landed promotions thanks to the smoker network (though this might be rationalizing the addiction!).

What's the power of the smoker network? A cigarette break could bring together the intern, the middle manager, and the executive; and employees from marketing, finance, or human resources within a given organization. Smokers are men, women, and members of every race—in contrast to the predictable web of similar and familiar contacts with whom people unconsciously surround themselves. Because smokers come from all different parts of an organization but regularly meet in one place where they can chat informally and share their different perspectives, they're able to capture a bird's-eye view of the firm.

We're certainly not recommending that managers start a caffeine or smoking habit. But you can foster the same sort of contact—just spend at least fifteen minutes each day walking a different path (even using a different bathroom or elevator) to stimulate unplanned conversations with new people. Despite all the time and money spent planning formalized interactions in networking events, assigning boundary spanners, and purchasing idea-sharing software, bridges can often form by far simpler, emergent processes.

Why are emergent interactions so powerful in capturing novel signals? There are two answers—and they go beyond the fact that face-to-face interaction tends to involve deeper conversations than online networking.

FREE CHOICE = NARROW CLIQUES. The first reason why emergent interactions yield novel signals is because they remove free choice. On the surface, "choice" seems like it's an advantage. But choice is precisely what traps people in preexisting silos and redundant noise when they choose who they friend on Facebook and whom they interact with at corporate events.[21] Because communication is largely an unregulated resource, people narrow too much— for instance, preferring to huddle in comfortable cliques rather than strike up awkward small talk with people they've never met before in face-to-face corporate networking events. By contrast, smoker networks or the people who happen to bump into each other during coffee breaks often do not represent a stratified subsection of the organization. They're instead people from all areas of the organization who are simply united by the surface feature of being a smoker or coffee drinker. You can't plan in advance who you may see—but you can take advantage of talking to someone new once you're there.

GEOGRAPHY STILL COUNTS. The second reason why people taking a coffee or cigarette break are more likely to capture signals is because they can break out of the geographic habits that tend to constrain their networking. Even if people don't choose those who are similar, they often still end up sitting in the same locations, walking the same footpaths, and inhabiting the spaces in the office where they are likely to bump into predictable people repeatedly. A smoking break or a coffee room chat, on the other hand, is a rare trip outside the silo, and it forces people into contact with a diverse cross-section of the firm.

As a personal experiment, Leigh changed her own footpath. Instead of taking the short, three-minute walk to her third-floor office, Leigh walked up to the sixth floor of her building and then snaked down the hallway of the fifth and fourth floors—occupied by colleagues that probably had not been on the third floor in more than a decade. On the fifth floor, she ran into a colleague who told her about a MOOC (Massive Online Open Course) project on operations research that he had just launched. Within five minutes, this led to a discussion about developing a MOOC on leadership, and a new course was born! This small change broke Leigh free from the Communication Trap and also created value, just by talking to a few new people.

Even though online technologies allow people to communicate across oceans in a split second, paradoxically, the volume and frequency of e-mails between any two people is still nearly entirely determined by their physical proximity.[22] A sociogram of Facebook users shows this tendency on a global scale. Using the service's data on friendship pairs, a Facebook intern, Paul Butler, merged it with "each user's current city and summed the number of friends between each pair of cities [then he] merged the data with the longitude and latitude of each city."[23] What emerged was not the usual cobweb of the sociogram—but a detailed x-ray where people's connections produced a skeletal system that was a nearly complete replica of the world map (with the exception of China and other areas where Facebook did not have significant presence). In Butler's words, "Not only were continents visible, certain international borders were apparent as well. What really struck me, though, was knowing that the lines didn't represent coasts or rivers or political borders, but real human relationships." Nevertheless, while the significant clustering is based on these boundaries of culture and language, there are also weaker lines that represent connection points between countries and across oceans. Just like the frogs in the pond, locality still siloes us, though the rarer ties that could bridge the oceans were also visible. To escape the echo chamber, people can't simply open up their social networking accounts, they need to move their physical selves around the organization!

Using Geography to Overcome Similarity

Geography and similarity are two "filters" that trap people in redundant noise. However, by claiming geography as a hidden resource, you can redesign (without regulating) communication networks to overcome networking based on similarity.

Tanya and researchers Arjun Chakravarti and Chris Winship studied the power of geography to break down racial affinities in a study at Harvard.[24] Specifically, Harvard freshmen are randomly assigned to live with roommates of different races so that they have the opportunity to interact with each other over the course of a year. After that period of close, productive, long-term interaction, people of different races were just as likely to continue to live together in the second year as same-race pairs in nearly all room configurations. Rather than spending significant time and money preaching the value of diversity in trainings, the college designed a simple and geographic head start, which spurred deep, long-term relationships that wiped out racial preferences in most group configurations.

How might this strategy apply to organizational silos? To encourage bridging ties, try randomly assigning seats at lunches, corporate events, and even meetings to mix up groups and break up the predictable coalitions. While assigning seats may seem better suited to elementary school, we found that even MBA students, when choosing their own seats, choose to be closer to classmates who are similar and familiar in terms of gender, ethnicity, and nationality. As awkward as you might feel as the leader who's assigning seats, the power of this technique lies in the fact that it's far more awkward for strangers to initiate interactions with each other. But once an accidental contact is initiated, people engage in small talk, laying the groundwork for deeper conversations and perhaps ultimately a relationship—even though people would have never initiated that relationship on their own.

Consider researcher Sandy Pentland's studies of people's communication patterns. He collected data using electronic ID badges capable of measuring who was talking to whom, for how long, how close they were standing, tone of voice, and so on. His findings indicated that whereas planned social events like "beer meets" had little effect on communication patterns, simply making the company's lunch tables longer (allowing more people to sit together) transformed communication because more accidental contacts could occur between strangers.[25]

When managers rethink how to leverage underutilized common spaces in their workplace, they create hubs that allow people throughout the organization to collide, prompting cross-departmental conversation and bridging ties. For instance, one of us worked in a business school in which the mailboxes were located on each department's floor, so that chance meetings between members of different departments never occurred. Additionally, the coffee room charged for drinks. Even though it was just a quarter, people preferred to stop over at a nearby coffee shop, and they rarely met colleagues from other departments.

By contrast, her previous university had a single mailroom that contained all faculty mailboxes. Each faculty member had to enter that mailroom at least once a day, and it became a hub where people had random collisions with those in diverse fields. These in turn spilled over into great conversations and idea exchange.

Even though communication was unregulated, this floor plan capitalized on people's natural footpaths. People had no choice but to get their mail. (The fact that the mailroom was stocked with free coffee of course helped!) Yet, as they mixed across departments, that interaction *felt* far less forced than those expensive "optional" office parties and awkward organization-sponsored networking events that people groan about and attend. By finding *underutilized common spaces* and putting them to work, you can create "random" collisions through smart design in a relatively inexpensive way.

Other CEOs have modified their own footpaths. Rather than isolating themselves in private suites in the corner of the office, they're taking the "middle seat" that maximizes their connectivity. For example, if you visit the corporate offices of Crate & Barrel, you will find the CEO, COO, and VP all in the middle of the room, which breaks down geographic barriers and allows them to be a part of impromptu conversations. Elevators are few and far between, but wide, grand staircases bring people of all levels together.

Even if you can't tear down your office's elevators, take a different staircase or try a different bathroom in the office—and encourage your employees to do that same. Then see how that simple change in your daily footpath widens your networks.

Bring Diversity to Your People

By finding two disconnected worlds and bringing them together—that is, bridging the structural hole—managers set the stage for creativity. A manager at Amazon.com, for example, contacted us because she was hoping to encourage more creative problem solving on her teams and wanted to hire a facilitator. They had organized weekly lunches where her project team would meet and informally discuss their issues. She had essentially designed a lunchtime echo chamber. Instead of spending the money on a facilitator, we suggested, why not just bring another team into the mix to inject a new perspective at every meeting?

Leigh and Hoon-Seok Choi tested this intervention in dramatic fashion. They created brainstorming groups, and in half of them, they systematically uprooted one team member and inserted a new member. It may sound inefficient, but the groups that had one member replaced with another were more creative than the groups without membership change.[26] New group members acted as catalysts, inspiring old members with new ideas. In short, newcomers brought out the best in "old-timers," connecting two previously unconnected worlds.

To fight the power of bonding ties, be deliberate about finding a voice that's likely to be truly fresh. Pick someone you don't know, or someone who's in a competing group, or someone who your first impressions indicate is irrelevant—or perhaps someone you don't even like. These are the voices that you are least likely to turn to as you think about people who could help. But they are the ones who are also likely to give your team the best mental workout.[27] The person you don't know or think is irrelevant may come with completely different assumptions and expose you to ideas you never considered before. The person who you don't like or compete with has arrows of criticism pointed right at your work, which could challenge your thinking. While most people avoid this mental and social exercise, creating an interaction that normally would never have existed, given your conventional footpaths and comfort zone, can make your ideas smarter and stronger.

Change the Conversation

Sometimes diversity is not something to be discovered outside your group—you already have it but don't use it! The solution doesn't lie in walking further but in thinking more broadly. An executive shared a particularly frustrating episode with us recently. A company that he desperately wanted a job with had an opening. He submitted his résumé—and never heard back. Months later, he ran into a friend who had worked in that industry for years and knew the hiring manager who would have screened his résumé. He had not looked at his own network broadly enough and now regretted it bitterly.

We've studied how people squander the value present in their own networks in various studies with organizational researcher

Ned Smith.[28] One of the things we observed is that people vary in their abilities as *network activators*. Consider Joe, for instance, who's an introvert rather than the stereotypical super-networker, but has an uncanny ability to sort through his mental rolodex on the spot and call on the right person to solve problems. Even if he's met a person for a single dinner, he'll remember what they care about—and file that information away to call on them as the need arises.

Beyond simply remembering his ties, Joe is also comfortable in calling on people—in contrast to others who exhibit what we call *network choking*. Just as athletes can choke on physical performance and test-takers can choke cognitively, people also choke socially, failing to get in touch with certain contacts because of social anxieties. It's simply awkward to call a boss from a decade ago out of the blue. And it's similarly challenging for people to contact someone who they know only a little—the other person might reject them or perhaps not even remember them. It's just easier to keep mining from the same set of people who feel comfortable. Our research indicates that the key is to approach these interactions with a psychological state that involves positive feelings—being happy, secure, and unthreatened—so you feel confident picking up the phone and exploring beyond your cliques.[29]

Another skill lies in people's conversational habits. Even if you're face-to-face with someone carrying a high-value signal, this doesn't mean you'll capture it. Most groups, even those composed of diverse members, gravitate toward a common denominator—a phenomenon known as the *common information effect*. They don't share new information, and prefer to talk about their shared knowledge. Because people fixate on their similarities, they fail to share and combine their unique information, and they lose the chance to learn from each other and find novel solutions.[30] These patterns manifest even in life-or-death situations. When medical professionals do not share "unique" information, this leads to an increase in incorrect diagnoses.[31]

Being aware of the common information effect is not enough to mitigate its effects. You also have to design conversations that overcome it. One strategy is known as *brainwriting*.[32] Before meeting as a group, assign people pre-work to brainstorm key ideas and write them down to ensure that they've generated their own thoughts before they hear anyone else's. (We discuss brainwriting further in chapter 6.) When the group gets together, print out and share everyone's pre-work so as to not lose insights during the conversation. And once the conversation begins, map it out. In the typical conversation map, the discussion roams without much direction until people eventually start to focus on particular directions. This may occur for arbitrary reasons—perhaps because a high-status person affirmed an idea or because a particularly persistent group member repeatedly pushed it to the fore.

But instead of narrowing the discussion so soon, purposefully keep an eye on the broad scope of ideas on the map. For example, one manager we spoke to, an especially skilled discussion leader, always visually represented the group's discussion process. When the group would fixate on a small subset of ideas, she'd look over the entire conversational map, and particularly at threads that were dropped due to a lack of affirming follow-up from others. Then, she'd push people to discuss what was new and different, rather than simply bonding on the intuitions they shared and coalesced around.[33]

In the process, she ensured that ideas weren't simply pruned away due to forgetfulness, the personalities involved, or some other unintentional process.

Chaotic Noise

While staying within the clique creates redundant noise, scanning too broadly can generate chaotic noise.[34] As we described at the beginning of this chapter, people facing too much communication might find themselves overstimulated. The question then is how to ensure that the diversity we find provides useful signals but doesn't create distracting chaos. We'll describe some strategies to engage in disciplined search to reduce the costs of oversearching and chaotic distraction. Before we begin, however, let's consider the level of chaotic noise you and your team might be fighting against right now.

What's Your Signal-to-Noise Ratio?

To what extent do find yourself caught in the web of the Communication Trap? As a quick check, look at your e-mail inbox at the close of the business day. Count how many messages you received, including spam, junk mail, nonessential communications that did not require any action on your part. When we've polled the executives we work with, they reported receiving several hundred. Next, identify which messages are truly informative and high value (i.e., the signals). Divide this by the number of messages you received in total. Higher scores indicate that you are on the receiving end of a richer signal. Lower scores indicate that you are tolerating a lot of irrelevant information.

When we've surveyed executives, some indicated that less than 10 percent of their e-mails were of critical importance. Many complained that an embarrassing number were "run-on good-byes": "Thank you for sending the report"; followed by "Sure, no problem"; followed by "Great!"; followed by "Any time!"; followed by "Good to know"; and so on. In other words, a single request could spur about five to seven of such non-value-added e-mails.

As a second step, count how many of the messages you sent were absolutely critical or high importance. Divide this by the number of messages you sent in total. Higher scores indicate that you are on the producing end of a richer signal. Lower scores indicate that you are creating a lot of low-signal communications that yield non-value-added information.

Finally, compare your *receive* signal strength with your *send* signal strength. If you find yourself sending more noise (junk) than you are receiving, you're placing unnecessary attentional demands on your teams (and spending your valuable time and energy doing so). If you find yourself receiving more noise (junk) than you are sending, congratulations—but you still need to educate your team on how to improve their communication fidelity. If all of these ratios are too high for you to tolerate, your organization as a whole may be trapped in a culture of hypercommunication.

When people say that e-mail is costless, it's often because they ignore its Type II costs: the person-hours spent reading and writing or checking those e-mails, or the distractions caused by nonessential e-mails. The waste even spills over into face-to-face interaction. Executives also reported that e-mail exchanges frequently resulted in a conversation that began, "Did you get my e-mail?" and then recapped the message. These duplicative conversations about an e-mail that was already sent could last upward of fifteen minutes!

People also feel stressed by the constant expectation of communication. Technology has blurred the line between people's work and non-work lives: 60 percent of working Americans respond to personal communications during work hours and nearly 50 percent respond to work during personal time.[35] Managers are expected to be infinitely available to their colleagues, customers, and clients. If they don't reply to e-mails immediately, they describe being chastised with curtly worded follow-ups: "*Maybe you didn't get this the first time, but I am requesting . . .*" This happens even when people are out of the country, on their honeymoons, or dealing with a sick child. And this is just the noise created by e-mail alone—we haven't even considered the many other gadgets on physical desktops and applications on computer desktops.

Let's consider two strategies for escaping these high-noise environments. The first lies in having *stopping rules* for controlling the automatic and relentless search for information; the second involves carving out complete but temporary escapes from technology—where you can find your focused flow of work, rather than being inundated by noisy information.

From the Dustbowl to the Vault

Dustbowl empiricism refers to the practice of steeping yourself in as much data as possible and analyzing all of it in hope of finding insights. In the era of big data, it's no surprise that we're facing an onslaught of information. Now, as people face tough problems, they find themselves asking for more, more, more. But most managers don't need more communication and information; they need better ways of sorting, categorizing, and analyzing the data they have.[36] After all, there will always be more information, resources, and perspectives to collect if you're willing to spend the time and money to gather it. As people engage in hypercommunication and gather more and more information, they can fly straight into a dustbowl rather than a vault.

One senior executive described how his boss, the company's CFO, sent employees on expensive quests for information. In part, she was cerebral and liked having all the information to understand a given situation, a good quality for a thoughtful decision maker. But she was also hesitant to make difficult decisions (what some might call "analysis paralysis"). Her knee-jerk response to the discomfort of decision making was to ask for more data as a crutch. These requests set off a chain reaction among the people below her who were forced to commit their time and resources to search for various data points and then perform fresh analyses on the ever-expanding data set. In substituting data gathering for analysis and continually delaying decision making, the CFO needlessly consumed organizational resources to buy information that muddied the problems rather than clarifying them.

There are clear costs then when people undersearch or oversearch in problem solving.[37] A classic puzzle in decision theory that models this trade-off is known as the *secretary problem*. An executive is seeking to hire an assistant. She meets candidates sequentially and has to decide then and there whether to accept them or reject them. Overly rapid acceptance can lead to "settling" on a suboptimal secretary. Overly cautious rejection can produce regrets from turning down superior alternatives.

The secretary problem has (of course) been applied to marriage markets. Stop too early, and you may be settling for a suboptimal match. Wait too long, you're getting older and missing out on good matches, who've now settled down with other people. Even though astronomer Johannes Kepler lived four hundred years before online dating, he still experienced the same overload as the frog in the pond as he searched for prospective brides. He kept detailed profiles of them: one had bad breath and another spent too much money. He found one he liked, but he also wanted to keep searching through his list in case he liked any others better.[38]

In essence, the CFO had the same issue. She had data but couldn't draw the line to ascertain whether it was the right data for the decision at hand. Her searches kept spiraling, bringing in more and more communication that wasted her time, energy, and money and failed to improve her decision making.

Mathematicians modeling this problem have formulated a precise 36.5 percent stopping rule; that is, if you have a pool of ten candidates, make no offers to anyone in the first 36.5 percent (basically the first four candidates) to sample the quality of the pool, and then select the one who's better than the best of that first set of four. This rule can curtail indefinite search.[39]

The mathematician's magic 36.5 percent number may be precise, but it doesn't help when the set of information you've got to sort through is virtually limitless. Though he lived long before the age of big data, British philosopher William of Occam offers a tip to discipline information search in practice. He observed that parsimonious decisions—those based on fewer variables and assumptions—tend to be more successful than those based on many contingencies. The principle of Occam's razor argues that you should cut away those concepts, variables, or constructs and make decisions based on simplicity and limited variables.

Asking three key questions at team meetings can help enforce the habit of disciplined information search and finding the right signals in the noise:

"What am I going to do with these data once I get them?" The CFO's massive data collection efforts signaled that work was being done, but it was action without traction that yielded few signals. Clarifying to yourself what data are actually *for* forces you to adopt Occam's razor as a governing principle, pushing you to edit out searches that don't help you frame your problem or understand it more clearly.

"If I don't get the information, will my decision change?" This question, an inversion of the previous one, pushes you even harder to determine how valuable certain data is to making a decision. It helps ensure that you're collecting data that tests a concrete hypothesis. Try to generate specific if/then statements: "If the revenues of this company are below $10 million per year, then it doesn't make sense for us to pursue the deal." If you already know the company's revenue is below $10 million, this clear statement helps you stop looking because finding any more information won't change your plans. If you hold yourself to the standards of testable hypotheses, employees who are charged with searching for and analyzing information will be happier simply because they'll understand why they're doing what they're doing, and you'll come to more effective (and faster) decisions.

"What will we have to forgo by committing this time and money to data collection?" As tempting as it can be to buy data, try to "think frugally" to help clarify your priorities: Would the data be worth purchasing if money was scarce? When comparing the thought processes of the poor and the rich, research indicates that poor people are better able to activate trade-offs.[40] This is because they are more practiced at exerting financial self-control as compared to the well off. Purchasing decisions that the wealthy can base entirely on preference, such as buying dinner, require rigorous trade-off calculations for the poor. They are used to having to make do with less and so they can fluidly envision opportunity costs in their decision-making. By activating trade-off thinking, people can recognize the (Type II) opportunity costs of unnecessary data collection and eliminate that waste.

Screening Out Distraction

The other part of eliminating the chaos of overcommunication involves carving out spaces that are free from chronic overstimulation.

Constantly checking e-mail and jumping between projects takes a toll on people's cognitive resources and productivity. People think they're "choosing" when they click on a website. But their attention is in fact being directed by carefully designed clickbait that guides them from click to click. When the average person breaks his or her chain of thought to go online—whether it's to network or read a nonessential e-mail—it takes sixteen minutes to recover focus.[41] Because online networking involves a continuous moment-to-moment distraction through the day (unlike coffee breaks), people are continuously cycling between productive work and unproductive online activities that disrupt their ability to focus.

One way to counteract technological multitasking waste is to relabel it. The word *multitasking* implies that it's super-productive—people can do multiple things at once! But it's far more accurate to think of it as *zerotasking*, because, in reality, doing many things at once means doing nothing well and wasting time and energy in the process. Psychological research indicates that when people multitask, they're in fact rapidly *switching* attention from one thing to another and back again. According to a Microsoft study, since 2000, the human attention span fell from twelve to eight seconds. That's a lower attention span than a goldfish (which can focus for a full nine seconds)![42] Whether it's texting while driving or texting while walking over a cliff, "zerotaskers" are cognitively compromised. In one study, while students using their laptops in class took more word-for-word notes about the lecture (because typing is faster than writing), they were cognitively compromised—performing worse in tests of conceptual understanding than students who took notes by hand.[43] Other studies have found that students using laptops spend about 40 percent of class time using it for purposes unrelated to class work, with some studies finding that 60 percent of students are distracted for half the class.[44]

The concept of flow stands in direct contrast to being inundated with information and rapidly switching attention between different tasks.[45] *Flow* is the captivating feeling of being fully focused on and absorbed in the task at hand to the point that nothing else matters. These are the moments where you are fully absorbed in your work—and creating value in the process—instead of being mindlessly directed from site to site by an advertiser's clickbait or the moment-to-moment demands of your inbox.

To create the conditions at work that enable flow, one organization began with tech-free meetings. This was highly unpopular at first, but people began to pay attention to their colleagues rather than checking e-mail and skimming the latest industry headlines. This resulted in better conversations and more efficient meetings.

Another policy is to afford people some protection from both technological and human interruptions by guaranteeing them at least one hour per day of uninterrupted work time. As challenging as it is to create without meetings or e-mails, it eliminates overstimulation and allows your team to work in a more focused way.

Finally, take the pressure off of people to respond to each e-mail within seconds. The ping of an incoming message has trained people to stop what they're doing and answer right away, interrupting their focus *and* causing their replies to be less thoughtful than they should be. Encourage your team to take the time they need for a better response and even suggest that they hold off answering all nonessential e-mails until the last hour of the workday. As we'll discuss more in chapter 6, when you design quiet time into work, people can escape from the noise and refocus.

Conclusion

The Communication Trap is everywhere in noisy talk, e-mails, tweets, and posts. In spite of all of the information people can access, they aren't any more efficient at capturing high-value signals. Instead, technology is often just adding more noise—both from ineffective communication and from overstimulation—that makes high-value signals even harder to distill.

To escape the Communication Trap, design higher-signal/lower-noise interactions that expose you and your teams to new ideas and that capture meaningful signals. What holds people back from doing so is not technology but psychology. People can connect with the world in a second, but still prefer those who are nearby, familiar, and similar because it's more psychologically comfortable to pattern interactions in these ways. They miss high-value signals as a result.

This chapter has identified inexpensive designs and best practices that set the stage for encounters between diverse people—whether it's random seating assignments, changing your footpaths, changing your conversational patterns to reveal what's new and unique versus what's shared, or using common spaces to allow for interaction that breaks through typical barriers such as geography, race, gender, and status. These strategies help you escape from the action without traction that arises from hearing the same conversations repeatedly. But it also creates risks from chaotic overcommunication. By controlling the hunger for constant information, whether that's through data searches or online connection, you can create spaces that sharpen your focus and enable higher-value work. And, as we'll see in chapter 6, to extract value from diverse interactions without having them descend into chaos—you have to also be prepared to coordinate those interactions as well.

CHAPTER 6

The Macromanagement Trap

When the Olympic Committee allowed NBA superstars to participate in Olympic basketball, it seemed like a Team USA victory would be a done deal every year. In Barcelona's 1992 Olympic Games, Team USA featured Michael Jordan, Magic Johnson, and Larry Bird. It was like "Elvis and the Beatles playing together," according to head coach Chuck Daly.[1] The "Dream Team" was bigger, stronger, more famous, more talented than any other, and their market value exceeded everyone else's. Even players from other countries mobbed them for autographs. The dream team would play to roaring crowds with pregame dunk shows, while the opposing teams quietly practiced their free throws on the other side. The talent level was so far beyond the other teams' that they merely needed to exert a bit of energy for a stretch, then cruise the rest of the game to win at blowout margins. What bookie in Las Vegas would take the bet on smaller countries with less experience and star power?

Fast-forward to 2004 in Athens. This team of superstars, which included MVPs such as LeBron James, Tim Duncan, and Allen Iverson, came to be known as the "Nightmare Team."[2] Tiny Puerto Rico handed the US team their first-round loss—at 92–73, the most lopsided loss in Team USA's history. Subsequent losses to Lithuania and Argentina completed the embarrassment. Sometimes, teams can cruise by on their individual raw talent, but that's not always enough. However brilliant your people may be, they may still struggle to get traction on their collective efforts.

Managers face similar challenges when they find that their product design teams, cross-functional teams, and sales teams deliver less than the sum of their parts. Consider the blowup of Long-Term Capital Management.[3] John Meriwether, formerly Salomon Brothers' vice chairman and head of bond trading, founded the hedge fund and assembled a finance version of the Dream Team. Despite their star power, this group of Nobel laureates and leading traders from Salomon managed to lose $4.5 billion—at a time when the average Joe investing in the market was making money. And worse, because they lacked tight controls, they took on so much risk that they nearly brought the entire financial system to the brink of ruin as well. In spite of their intellectual horsepower, the team's results were catastrophic, and tremendous talent was squandered.

It makes perfect sense to recruit teams with exceptional talent. And very often, that strategy succeeds. But as managers hire the best people, sit back, and wait for the magic show, they can fall straight to the Macromanagement Trap—the faulty belief that simply assembling talented people and allowing them free rein will result in synergistic, value-creating performance.[4] When a signal encounters an opening or free space, it breaks down and spreads to different directions. In the same way, macromanagers create vacuums that leave their groups stuck in uncoordinated action.

The temptation to stay out of the way of employees can be strongest when leading really talented people and superstars. However, as the Nightmare Team and as the Long-Term Capital episodes suggest, collections of superstars may in fact need *more* structure and management rather than less.

But even if a team doesn't consist of individual superstars, macromanagement still squanders its true value. One executive described how his CEO empowered two up-and-coming vice presidents to take charge of a multimillion-dollar project: developing a new regional office. They were supposed to collaborate, but they had interpersonal issues. So they divided up the responsibilities to minimize their actual interaction. One was primarily in charge of the initial build, and other would step in to oversee the project's final stages. The CEO granted them full autonomy through the entire process.

While one manager spent most of his time onsite directing and planning the project, the other was only passively engaged via occasional updates. A month before the office's grand opening, the absentee manager discovered several critical oversights and blamed the onsite manager. The CEO who had let out the leash failed to create empowered managers: he instead created frustrated employees who floundered without support and direction, costing the company several hundred thousand dollars to rework the building.

Another executive described his boss, who would hastily set up committees when faced with problems, hoping that they'd generate some insight. There were called "task forces," "town halls," "working groups," and "strategic deep dives," but behind each of these euphemisms was an unstructured committee that would sink hours on unfocused discussions that yielded no tangible results. We call this illusion that groups can automatically generate value the *multiply-by-zero fallacy*. You put five people with zero ideas on a committee for twenty man-hours and you're still going end up with zero ideas—*and* negative twenty hours. Indeed, various apps now allow managers to track the financial cost of each meeting by considering the number of people attending, their job titles, and estimated salary.[5]

Why People Get Caught in the Macromanagement Trap

Several key managerial strengths can become liabilities that ensnare people in the Macromanagement Trap. First, most leaders strongly endorse "empowering" employees, "delegating," and being "hands-off." They express a profound trust in their employees' talent and capabilities to do independent work. Indeed, the managers we have worked with are rarely micromanagers. They don't have the time or desire to hover over employees and monitor their every move. And the idea of increasing their team's effectiveness by decreasing their own workload is admittedly appealing. But in avoiding micromanagement, managers might allow their style to swing too far in the other direction.

Second, managers can fall into the Macromanagement Trap in a well-meaning effort to avoid the Communication Trap. In chapter 5, we described how managers can escape from silos and overdesigned technologies by creating free-form spaces that encourage face-to-face contact between diverse people. But, as people come together in collaboration, this can create noisy chaos if interactions are poorly coordinated. The challenge lies in developing teams that simultaneously broaden their contacts and drill down in well-aligned processes that facilitate implementation.[6] In spite of the real-time dynamism that can occur when people talk, think, and create together in person, many face-to-face interactions become wasteful when they are underdesigned and poorly coordinated. The hands-off approach fails to provide the scaffolding necessary to structure teams, missions, and deliverables.

Third, executives can also fall into the Macromanagement Trap precisely because they become frustrated with wasteful bureaucracies—too many rules, procedures, and hierarchical levels. Indeed, various innovative businesses have experimented with "undressing" their organizations. In the most extreme examples, some organizations have flattened the organization and even eliminated top-down controls over employees altogether.

One example is that of Zappos's *holacracy.*[7] This term refers to "a new way of running an organization that removes power from a management hierarchy and distributes it across clear roles, which can then be executed autonomously, without a micromanaging boss."[8] You might assume that everyone would be thrilled to learn that they no longer had a boss. People certainly complain about hierarchies and the micromanagers who exert control within them. For instance, an Accountemps survey found that 59 percent of employees have worked for a micromanager during their careers, and of those, 68 percent reported reduced morale, and 55 percent experienced reduced productivity.[9] The problem is that when companies take out the bureaucracy and don't fill in the gap, they're left with undercoordinated teams. As much as people dislike rules and hierarchy, they also dread uncertainty, and hierarchy eliminates various kinds of uncertainties in coordinating work and managing accountability.[10]

Studies show that well-designed teams with poor leaders are more successful than poorly designed teams with charismatic leaders, precisely because the norms and expectations were clear.[11] Management guru Frederic Laloux, whose writing helped inspire Zappos's transformation, observes that there's in fact *more* structure in successful self-managing organizations—it's just differently organized.[12]

The trend of subtraction and less-is-more imperatives can potentially eliminate the process losses from hierarchies at companies such as Zappos. But when macromanagers simply remove structure without filling in the gaps, they risk creating new process losses as people fill the vacuums by adding in structures of their own, which can also wipe out opportunities for potential process gains. Consider the simple equation that researcher Ivan Steiner proposed to express how much value is created—and lost—in groups:[13]

$$AP = PP - PL + PG$$

In this model, AP is the actual productivity of a group. PP refers to potential productivity—what the group members *could* achieve if they were able to effectively combine their talents. PG refers to process gain, or the synergistic, multiplicative advantages that could accrue when people come together.

But there's also the negative side. PL refers to process loss—what the group loses through their interactions. Process losses occur in two ways:[14]

- Motivation loss: Decreased productivity due to people lacking motivation in groups—for example, free riders failing to contribute (as discussed in chapter 3).

- Coordination loss: Decreased productivity due to poor group organization (including unproductive conversations, failures to use people's expertise, and miscommunication). While free riders may attract the lion's share of attention in groups, coordination losses can silently leak significant value.

Most leaders focus on a group's potential, and then sit back and relax. It's easier to focus on the figure (i.e., individual group members and their capabilities) while missing the ground (i.e., the stage that managers set, which determines whether the group can minimize its process losses and realize its process gains).

The bottom line is that effective *group process* is the key predictor of a team's success. It is the missing variable that explains whether people placed together will be able to create value or squander it. As we'll see, the solution to the Macromanagement Trap is not to micromanage but rather to set the ground rules for team success by strategically coordinating people's individual actions so that their collective actions gain traction. We'll begin by exploring the example of brainstorming groups, which so often expose the dangers of macromanagement, and consider smart designs to minimize the process losses. We'll then consider how teams can cycle between working in the "cave" and "commons" to tap the powers of both individual and group work. Finally, we'll consider techniques managers can use to leverage conflict and become more cohesive. The key message: *Don't control or abdicate—coordinate.*

Redesign Brainstorming to Boost Your Collective Brainpower

Brainstorming sounds great in theory. The group's creativity is unleashed and countless new ideas spontaneously emerge. Unfortunately, nearly every analysis of brainstorming over the past sixty years has found that a brainstorming group produces fewer and lower-quality ideas than the same number of people working alone. Brainstorming is a perfect example of a business strategy that feels great, but doesn't look so great when we consider the actual evidence of its effectiveness.[15] How could this be?

Brainstorming as it's often practiced involves free-form spaces and freewheeling discussions that clearly expose the pitfalls of macromanagement. When marketing executive Alex Osborn coined the term *brainstorming* in 1948, people were looking for ways to create together, and the brainstorming concept provided just that interface. While most executives report participating in brainstorming sessions that lack any ground rules whatsoever, Osborn in fact established four ground rules of brainstorming:

- Quantity: Generate lots of ideas—because quantity leads to quality.

- Building: Connect related ideas.

- Expressiveness: Share any idea without self-censorship.

- No criticism: No judgments about ideas—i.e., blame, feasibility, etc.

While research has proven the wisdom of the first two ideas—generating lots of ideas and connecting them to others' ideas—the last two principles have received less validation in research.[16] First, expressiveness tilts the conversation in favor of high-status people and extroverts who fill the vacuum with talk, causing groups to lose the collective wisdom of the introverts and less powerful voices. Meanwhile, process losses accumulate as others sit back and free ride—often conforming to first and loudest ideas introduced.

Further, criticism of ideas—but not the people offering the ideas—actually *improves* the outcome by encouraging creative tension.[17] Studies of groupthink, for example, describe the dangers of particular self-appointed *mindguards*, who shield the group from diverse perspectives by pushing for consensus.[18] They may urge the group to make decisions quickly or pressure the group to come to particular outcomes, driving the group straight into an Agreement Trap by shutting down creative conflict.

Rather than throwing the creative baby out with the brainstorming bathwater, let's consider new ground rules and designs to coordinate your group's interactions and improve their "collective brain":

Brainwriting

When we facilitate corporate off-sites, we are often warned that dominant alpha managers will try to monopolize the group. To deal with conversational monopolists and ensure that all ideas are heard, we use a proven technique called *brainwriting*.[19] Rather than go head-to-head with such individuals to try and silence them, a more effective plan of attack is to amplify the other participants. At the start of the session, we pass out hundreds of index cards and ask everyone to write down their ideas, without listing their names. After about ten minutes, the group has generated hundreds of (anonymous) ideas. Then the group votes on the ideas (again, anonymously). The anonymity prevents peer pressure and also masks the messenger's charisma, likeability, persistence, or power to affect these processes. This way, the group can leverage the ideas of the dominant members, but in a way that allows other ideas to be heard as well.

Research indicates that brainwriting allows people to generate more ideas than traditional brainstorming—in one study, more than twice as many.[20] One reason for this is that verbalizing ideas creates production blocking; that is, when one person is talking, everyone else's idea generation is interrupted, slowing the group down and causing people to forget ideas they had in mind.[21]

You can also use this exercise for a group spread over multiple locations. Just move the discussion online. As we discussed in chapter 5, when overused, online communications are likely to degrade the signal-to-noise ratio. However, in this case, online brainstorming can outperform face-to-face brainstorming! Why? Online brainstorming is effectively a form of brainwriting, which eliminates the process losses from talk. Online chats can also facilitate anonymity by disguising usernames to reduce bias toward particular messengers. It's a natural option for virtual meetings and teams.

The Wisdom of Crowds

Additionally, consider techniques to scan widely for solutions—so that you can harness the wisdom of even crowds that seem to be impossible to coordinate as a group. By polling and averaging the collective opinion of hundreds of people, you can identify a more accurate signal than any one individual's. As on Yelp.com's ratings of restaurants and shops, the evaluation of one idiosyncratic negative reviewer is canceled out by the one who had the unusually good experience. Thus, ten thousand people broadly dispersed in the company should theoretically offer a more accurate prediction of the company's growth prospects than one or two key decision makers—even (or perhaps, especially) if they are sitting in the C-suite.[22]

Even though the crowd appears to be uncoordinated—indeed, people are working independently, so there's no chance of process losses from collaboration—techniques such as brainwriting and wisdom of crowds work because they offer significantly more coordination in terms of collecting and combining the collective wisdom of members than macromanagers do when leading face-to-face groups. When face-to-face groups are undermanaged, they are easily commandeered by certain high-status members, such that others tend to quickly conform to those opinions and hidden experts are overlooked. By simply pooling the full range of knowledge from the collective and evaluating solutions—ideally, anonymously—the crowd can often outperform face-to-face groups.

As one example, software developer Eric Raymond's book *The Cathedral and the Bazaar* contrasts the cathedral model (source code is available with each release, and elites develop code between releases) and the bazaar (the code is open source, and the public can view the code online). The bazaar dominates due to what Raymond calls Linus's law (after Linus Torvalds, the leader of the Linux kernel project): "Given enough eyeballs, all bugs are shallow." More people seeing the code means a higher likelihood of catching the bug.

In fact, the bazaar model—along with the "gamification" principle (turning work into games and contests)—facilitated problem solving in a complex scientific challenge. The "protein folding problem" is known as one of the 125 most compelling scientific conundrums. The irregularities in the folding of proteins underlie a vast array of diseases: certain cancers, cystic fibrosis, and Alzheimer's, Parkinson's, and Creutzfeldt-Jakob disease. To advance in solving this problem, scientists need to understand the rules that govern the shape that the protein will adopt. So, in 2010, University of Washington biochemists and computer scientists created a game called "Foldit."[23] It required people to use their spatial skills to manipulate the proteins in folds that would earn them the greatest number of points. Fifty-seven thousand gamers participated, and the humans outperformed computers on five out of ten puzzles and achieved similar results on three.[24] In other words, by giving more people access to the problem (and even making a game out of it), and collecting and exploiting their ideas, there's a higher likelihood of finding the solution—even if people are not all in the same room.

Brainswarming

While brainwriting and the wisdom of crowds can help aggregate the inputs of individuals working alone, a newer technique uses the metaphor of swarming ants to reorganize how people creatively function in face-to-face interactions around a problem. Just as ants leave signals (in the form of pheromones), *brainswarming* also eliminates the need for talk. It uses a visualization exercise to build and hone in on ideas as a team. With this technique, you create a board with the goal on top, and available resources on the bottom. Participants attach notes to the board, with top-down thinkers refining the goal, and bottom-up thinkers adding more resources and ways to use them, until the paths converge—swarming to a solution. Studies reveal that brainswarming yields up to 60 percent more ideas than traditional brainstorming.[25]

Verbal Idea Generation

To eliminate the steep process losses resulting from talk, these alternatives to traditional brainstorming eliminate talk in both generating and evaluating ideas. But sometimes face-to-face conversations are necessary. If you are designing a face-to-face verbal idea-generation session, consider implementing two ground rules that reduce process losses from talk:

- Vertical takeoff: A key factor that limits the number of ideas generated during brainstorming is the length of each individual contribution. One of us uses a warm-up before brainstorming exercises called the *vertical takeoff.*" It involves people having a two-minute conversation with a colleague in which they immediately get to the point. We have found that people often "stall out" when starting a conversation. By using the vertical takeoff to encourage and train team members to express themselves more efficiently, you can dramatically increase your signal-to noise ratio—crucial in brainstorming meetings where productivity is strongly associated with the quantity—and therefore the eventual quality—of the ideas generated.

- Cut down horizontal trail-off: Another source of productivity loss is that people don't close off their comments succinctly, so a potentially useful idea can get lost as the speaker rambles on. One ground rule to curtail such *horizontal trail-off* is to seize it as an opportunity to bring in a quieter voice. If the speaker has run over the two-minute mark, a facilitator might step in and say, "Let me interrupt you—maybe it will help if we get other perspectives on this. We've not heard from Miranda, what does she think about it?"

None of these techniques requires you to monitor, control, or micromanage your group; instead, they allow you to set the stage for information exchange through new designs for interaction and constructive ground rules. But sometimes ground rules aren't enough: the real question is whether your people should be working in group settings at all. We now consider a technique that allows you to maximize the advantages of both public and private spaces.

The Cave and Commons

In 2013, Marissa Mayer of Yahoo! created a stir when she changed office policy and declared that employees would no longer be allowed to work from home. Mayer believed that being visible was key to establishing a learning culture.

A similar belief has also led several companies to dismantle all offices, and even cubicles, and put everyone in large, open spaces. This policy is controversial, but it raises an interesting question: Does constant cohabitation make groups more productive? If properly designed, it could allow for random collisions—but it could also create its own process losses through distraction.

In a study of software engineers, researchers found that 62 percent of top performers described their workspace as private, compared with 19 percent of poor performers. Furthermore, 76 percent of poor performers felt needlessly interrupted at work, while only 38 percent of the top performers did.[26] Clearly, software engineers who are involved in complex work need uninterrupted quiet time, away from distracting coworkers.[27]

But encouraging *too* much independent work can create other coordination problems in collaborative tasks and projects. For example, one Silicon Valley company decided to completely eliminate its weekly face-to-face meetings and conduct everything via e-mail. Rather than reducing inefficiency, this arrangement led to frequent miscommunications because the work was deeply collaborative and people missed critical nuances.

The problem is that companies create false choices between individual work and group work, when they should be improving how they deploy *both*. What's needed is a flexible transition between the *cave* (private space) and the *commons* (public space). When you're managing teams, you need the ambidexterity to know when to dial the group activity down and turn the individual activity up, and when to kick the groups into action again.

Balancing Cave and Commons

As a guideline, when your team's work requires focus, keep them in the cave, which is a low-signal/low-noise environment. A basic psychological principle is that alone time is especially important when individuals are performing nondominant (i.e., complex, novel) individual tasks, while the commons can facilitate dominant (easy, well-learned) individual tasks.[28] For instance, try to solve a complex math problem in the commons while an audience simply watches you. Even if they're not actively distracting you with talk, their mere presence creates arousal and becomes "nerves," interfering with your ability to focus on nondominant tasks. By contrast, running is a dominant, well-learned task. As many recreational joggers know, having other people around inspires runners to pick up their stride. For well-learned tasks such as running, the noise in the commons isn't disruptive—it's energizing and improves performance.

While people need their caves for an escape from the noise so they can be creative and get focused, the commons allows them to get clarification and buy-in on what the signal is. One manager described the rule of 3 × 3 in her organization whereby her team called a face-to-face meeting whenever they found themselves on e-mail chains that had more than three people and elicited a chain of more than three (verbose) e-mails. They could quickly check in face-to-face and clarify the issue—and then get back to the cave and work. Rather than organizing marathon two-hour weekly meetings (where more time may be spent discussing past performance than present concerns and goals), brief but frequent bursts of group work can unblock individual thinking. This dynamic provides the necessary infusion of new thinking and reduces people's sense of isolation and distance, while allowing people to rapidly cycle back to the cave to perform focused work.

Creating the Conditions for Groups to Coalesce

Once you've decided to deploy your people in groups, it's likely that you'll need more coordination than the bazaar. You may be managing teams that can't quickly divide the job into individual tasks and simply retreat to the cave. In these situations, your challenge is building a group that thinks and works as an organized unit.

The Olympic Nightmare Team, as well as the Dream teams, faced exactly this challenge. Even though these players were individually the best of the best, most of the year, they played on separate, competing NBA teams. They had hours of practice with the same teammates and had developed tacit knowledge about their playing style, competencies, and how to coordinate the interaction. As a recently brought-together team of stars, the Nightmare Team hadn't acquired the knowledge to work together, so all the efforts that went into bringing them together were squandered.

Researcher Sandy Pentland observed that when people explain how groups coalesce and achieve synergies, they often rely on illusory concepts like "the group clicked" or "there was a buzz." Pentland sought to provide answers that are more precise and quantifiable. Data he collected via electronic badges showed that the groups that coalesce exhibit energy (measured as frequent exchanges including conversations and nonverbal signals such as head nodding during interactions), engagement (distribution of energy among team members so that there is relatively equal contributions in the group rather than clusters who don't participate), and exploration (exchanges beyond the echo chamber of the group).

Rather than stepping aside and expecting the magic to happen, we'll now describe a series of tools to actively build this connective tissue between people so they can think and act like a productive and coherent group.[29]

Talking the Talk

A key step in building the connective tissue of a successful team is to develop a common language. Leigh's work with researcher Taya Cohen established that by simply talking about group processes, people gain an awareness of what they're doing together, and each person's role within the group.[30]

Metacognition, or thinking about thinking, doesn't need to be complicated. In fact, you can improve a group's performance by simply talking about how the group functions. In one study, researcher Anita Wooley created an experimental task where groups were given a series of clues, and had to use them to dismantle a hypothetical terrorist plot. In one condition, she offered an intervention. She began by identifying the unique talents that each possessed, and then asked them to discuss how to manage those talents.[31] As a next step, teams were given a worksheet that delineated the steps of the planning exercise. Teams were also given a ten-minute video that guided them through the steps. Members were then told to collectively review the types of evidence they were provided, assess member abilities and their relationship to the types of analyses that were involved, and then plan their approach to their analysis—allowing them to more effectively integrate information, structure the problem more effectively, and perform better than those who did not have the opportunity to think about how they would coordinate their abilities.

Because group members were able to understand each other's expertise, they could create process gains through synergies. Here is how synergy creation works: groups have to recognize each person's unique expertise. If each group member can contribute what he or she knows best (and allow others to contribute what they know best), the collective product will exceed what any single individual could do.

In chapter 5, we noted that inviting a newcomer into the team creates an influx of new ideas. The disruption also causes an internal reaction in the group. Specifically, team members spontaneously reflect on how the team works, which functions as a form of indoctrination or education. In fact, the process of team development generally begins with this critical period of socialization.[32] When group members step back from the business at hand and describe *how* they operate, they become thoughtful and observant. This cognition is a precursor to coordinated action.[33]

When we work with companies, we routinely ask the group how they make collective decisions. We have observed two consistent outcomes. First, group members have different views about how they do things. Second, they didn't realize that they had different views. As a case in point, we recently worked with a high-tech company that employed both engineers and sales and marketing people. When we asked the group how they made decisions, the engineers complained, "We often make decisions in the absence of evidence and we don't always ask the right questions." The salespeople had a completely different view of the collective decision-making process and expressed their frustration with being stymied by hundreds of reports, a mountain of data, and superfluous information. By the end of the afternoon, having exposed this disagreement, the group came up with a mutually agreed-upon plan for collective decision making.

Each of these interventions improves groups' performance by stimulating their metacognition—thinking about how they were thinking and working. But, while individual understanding of team dynamics can improve performance, it's the *interpersonal* behavior among team members that ultimately determines a group's success or failure.

Walking the Walk

In some situations, the way you coordinate your team could mean the difference between life and death. Suppose you need to assemble a surgical team for a major operation. Which of the following teams would you pick?

a. A team of doctors trained at top-ranked, Ivy League schools and highly qualified nurses and technicians.

b. The team that has frequently operated together before.

c. A team of the most senior doctors, nurses, and technicians.

As mundane as it appears, it turns out that option b is the best predictor of whether your surgery will be a success or failure. A study at Carnegie Mellon Hospital found that the outcome of knee- and hip-replacement surgeries could be almost entirely predicted by how many times the surgical team had worked together in the operating room.[34] Similarly, coal-mining accidents have been associated with how often the crew had worked together.[35] And a study of airline tragedies and malfunctions revealed that team experience was four times more important than pilot fatigue in predicting accidents.[36]

Why does working together as team matter? The reason lies in the team's mental models. When a musician's mental and the physical connections come together as he or she plays, it creates a literal neural symphony, lighting up multiple areas of the brain at the same time.[37] In the same way, an expert team creates a neural symphony—not just within individuals, but between them, as they acquire practice working as a team.[38] What this means specifically is that they acquire rich mental models that allow them to rapidly—and without a spoken word—recognize who knows what.

Consider one experiment, in which teams had to build transistor AM radios from kits. The task wasn't difficult, but it involved carefully following a detailed instruction manual. Some of the teams trained as a group and others trained individually. The next day, the experimenters took the instruction manuals away and asked the teams to rebuild the radios. The teams that had worked together the day before were able to successfully rebuild their radios by relying on the tacit cues and communication, the transactive memory system they had created the day before. However, the teams that were composed of members who had trained individually the day before were unable to rebuild the radios, even though the individual team members had the same amount of training. They were unsuccessful because they lacked a team mental model and had not built an implicit system as a team.[39] While individuals may be skilled and knowledgeable, educating people *as a group* provides the implicit collective knowledge that helps teams become more than the sum of their parts.

That's not to say you must use the same old team time and time again—chapter 5 already described the power of infusing your teams with new members and ideas. But rather than starting a team from the ground up, recognize the relationships and working processes already in existence by using a few familiar members who can create a foundation for more coordinated action.

From Conflict to Cohesion

By definition, "supergroups" are composed of superstars, and exclude the superstars' supporting cast. When managers assemble supergroups, they often assume that the individual stars alone are responsible for their own success. But without the supporting casts that help (and challenge) superstars, they would never have become as great as they are.

A supporting cast allows for complementarities. In contrast, supergroups inadvertently maximize noisy interference. That is, grouping superstars together—with the members each vying for the limelight and getting in each other's way—diminishes the effectiveness of each member and therefore the group as a whole. Simply telling the stars, "Now work together," ignores the natural competition between these players as they negotiate their place in the status hierarchy (as we saw with the Winner's Trap). Even if you're not leading a supergroup, you may still have prima donnas who are accustomed to star treatment.

Conflict is the ultimate interference effect, where people actively compete with fellow group members rather than setting the stage for their mutual success. As Sandeep learned all too well, coalitions—groups of people within a team who align themselves to achieve a goal or block an outcome—present a particular danger to group coherence.[40]

The Four Symptoms of Unproductive Conflict

Marriage psychologist John Gottman has a unique talent: he can watch a couple interact for just a few moments, and predict with over 90 percent accuracy whether that marriage will last or result in divorce. What's his secret? Is he a fortune-teller? Dr. Gottman and his colleagues identified four corrosive dynamics that are at the heart of all bad relationships.[41] They call these devastating sequences the "four horsemen of the apocalypse." These horsemen also ride into interpersonal dynamics at work and on teams, bringing pain without gains. Unlike the task conflicts we described in chapter 4, these are the conflicts that don't make you smarter and stronger—they make you angrier and more frustrated as they spiral into energy-sucking waste. The four horsemen are:

- Criticism: Critical statements blame the other person and label the other person as the problem—recall fundamental attribution errors in chapter 2 ("Mae, you are always difficult and inflexible."). Rather than framing criticism as blame, use "I" statements that focus on your perceptions of the situation ("I've observed that you don't like it when I propose these short-term technical tweaks. Can we talk about why this is?").

- Defensiveness: Defensive people respond to attack by deflecting blame and playing the victim ("Well, Rob, you're the one who should be communicating the product features better to the users"). The antidote to this poisonous sequence lies in accepting your part of the responsibility for the problem.

- Contempt: This third horseman is the most devastating—with a 95 percent association with divorce. Basically, it is implying that you are better than or smarter than your partner. Is a husband looking at his wife as though she is lucky to be with him? Is a wife rolling her eyes, sighing, and simply looking disgusted? By analyzing these micro expressions, or split-second behaviors, Gottman can make his prediction. On teams, a contempt spiral can be observed in eye rolling, as well as sarcasm, looking away, perhaps fiddling with a smartphone, when others are speaking. The antidote involves breaking down disrespectful norms and rebuilding interactions around mutual appreciation.

- Stonewalling or ignoring the other: Stonewalling is often the end result of all of the other behaviors. After repeated criticism, defensiveness, and contempt, it's a prelude to an end state where people lose faith in the ability to talk through issues in a meaningful way. The antidote lies in calming down, taking a timed break, and ultimately, finding a way to work through core issues.

While marriage may be far from your mind as you manage your teams, these same patterns play out in workplace groups as well. As you look for these patterns, ask: What are the triggers? Who instigates the criticism? Who gets defensive in response? And who's fully disengaged from the communication?

Then, rather than finding yourself locked in the same wasteful conversations for months or years, interrupt these sequences with the alternative sequence of action that Dr. Gottman proposes. Sandeep observed that a few specific arguments recurred on his team, consistently wasting time. The dynamic was invariably triggered when one group perceived that the other was "blaming" them. Once you've observed such a trigger, rather than getting sucked into wasteful spending, hijack the sequence. For instance, when the blame sequence began and the group started spiraling into conflict, Sandeep simply accepted responsibility for his own part in creating that problem. And when the two lead figures on either side reciprocated by accepting some responsibility as well, the usual dynamic was reined in. By recognizing these four patterns of escalation, you can steer conversations in more productive directions. These may be more easily said than done, but the alternative is getting trapped in a spiral of conflict and waste.

The Oddball Effect

Finally, let's think beyond interpersonal sequences in conflict to recognize the group-level patterns. Perhaps there are four people in your group, and no matter what the issue, the same people pair up on either side and derail decision making. You can predict who's going to say what and who is going to disagree with whom. Every day, you fixate on the same, circular, wasteful conversation where nothing gets accomplished. So, you spend thousands of dollars on pricy team-building excursions, only to return Monday morning to the same old dynamics. As a leader, how can you break through this hardened dynamic?

Managers are often preoccupied with perfecting the subtle complexities of group dynamics, and can overlook one very simple metric that can make a big difference: the number of people in the group. Specifically, is the group size odd or even? On the surface, this would seem to be irrelevant. However, the "odd-even" effect can dramatically affect group cohesion and collective decision making. Tanya's studies with researcher Kathy Phillips have shown that coalitions in odd-size groups are more likely to engage in hands-across-the water conversations and less likely to adopt unflinching stances. Simply put, odd-size groups are more cohesive than even-size groups.[42]

This conclusion may seem counterintuitive. After all, when people think about three-person groups, they imagine the dreaded two versus one dynamic, where one person is left out. In fact, subjects in our studies noted that they generally preferred even numbers precisely because they were balanced and symmetrical, while odd numbers were pointy and prime)! So why are odd-size groups more cohesive?

Ironically, the imbalance inherent in odd-size groups creates more cohesion. While even-size groups can split into equally powerful coalitions, odd-size groups encourage team members to make conclusive decisions. If people know that the outcome of a majority vote will produce a winner and loser, and that a stalemate cannot occur, they work harder to mobilize others in the group. Conversely, even-size group members can resign themselves to ongoing indecision.

How can this insight about odd-even help managers structure work? When you're managing a stalemated group, change the coalition structure by adding a few new members (or, if the group is already too large, removing a few). When Sandeep added a few independent members to his team, he observed that each coalition initially made a play for the new members, hoping to dominate the other side. But, eventually it became clear that they couldn't attract the new members by being extreme, difficult, and polarizing. So both sides gravitated to the center, and the new members helped bring the previously incompatible sides together.

Parkinson's Law

Once you've coordinated team members to think and act as a team, challenge them to work faster! Whether you know it or not, you probably experience Parkinson's Law almost every day. It states that work expands to fill the amount of time available for it.[43] While it may seem like a folksy aphorism, Parkinson's Law has been empirically validated: in one experiment, three groups were given a task to complete. One group was given one hour; the second, two hours; and the third, three hours. The depressing (but not surprising) finding was that all of the groups did approximately the same amount of work. They simply worked at a pace determined by the amount of time they had to fill![44] So, whenever you feel like an hour-long meeting could have taken fifteen minutes, you're probably right.

Looking deeper into this phenomenon, an interesting pattern emerges: Groups tend to perform inefficiently until the midpoint of their allotted time. Then, they kick into gear and get their work done just before the deadline.[45]

One way around this "eleventh-hour effect" is to set a deadline *before* the actual deadline, by which time all members will agree to reach a mutual understanding. Then use the remaining time to improve the outcome. In negotiations, this process can add 25 percent more value to the collective decision. Thus, if you are doing a $100,000 deal, you can deliver $25,000 more value!

Next time you schedule a meeting, try to shorten the allotted time and see how efficient your team can be. IDEO managers, for example, gave three project design teams only two hours to design a new office cubicle. Sure, they could have allocated two weeks, but in two hours, the group still achieved significant advances and started sharing ideas and mock-ups. The end result was a new cubicle composed of moveable blocks, so people could customize their workspaces.[46]

In addition to shortening your meetings, measure the outputs of each meeting whenever possible. Managers often organize off-sites to facilitate brainstorming or hire experts to facilitate meetings. After a long day of nonstop discussions, it feels like hard work has been done. But ask yourself a question: How many of the ideas generated in those meetings are acted on in the following two weeks (ideas tend to go dormant if not acted on in two weeks)? Think about your last off-site. How many ideas were actually put into action?

Conclusion

The Macromanagement Trap refers to the waste that ensues when managers assume that smart people working together in resource-rich organizations will figure things out and work in a productive, conflict-free manner. In an effort to be supportive and give their employees space to grow, develop, and come up with new ideas, they become too passive and teams fall apart. A group that was intended to be a dream becomes a nightmare, wasting time, money, and their own potential in the process.

Great teamwork and collaboration is neither about controlling people nor about delegating and waiting for people to spontaneously create magic together. It's about creating the right structures to coordinate your people and eliminate interference effects between them. Whether it is creating structured exercises to unleash better ideas, strategically cycling between individual and group work, or helping the group talk through their processes and navigate past conflict, you improve team performance through your managerial choices. Escaping the Macromanagement Trap isn't about becoming a micromanager—it's about providing the coordination required to transform individual stars into a truly super group.

CHAPTER 7

From Wicked Problems to Workable Solutions

Throughout this book, we've explored the spending traps that ensnare managers as they attempt to achieve their missions. When in these thorny traps, managers aren't making purposeful progress on their goals. They're trying to send and receive signals, but face noisy interference rather than clear transmission. They're investing their money, time, and energy in action, but end up losing the connection between their inputs and the results. When managers face action without traction, they're in a zone of maximum frustration.

The traps are especially insidious because, ironically, they often result from the skills and strengths that have served successful people so well in the past. The very talents that allow managers to excel in so many situations also set these spending traps in motion and frustrate even the most talented and motivated leaders. Thus, a simple insight lies at the heart of this book: to tame wicked problems and address the toughest problems, leaders and managers have to tame their own talents. When managers stop spending and start managing, they don't just save their time and money by getting traction on actions or even cutting the often-invisible corporate waste. They also discover their own limitless value.

The real challenge goes beyond recognizing the traps, and instead involves initiating a strategy to escape from them. The first step is to identify the critical places where the most resources are being invested without yielding the results you desire and expect.

Getting Started

Look back at the Daily Waste Score worksheet you filled out in chapter 1. Which areas had the biggest price tags? Hiring the wrong employees? Unmotivated employees? Resolving conflict? More to the point: Are your efforts in these areas producing the results you expect? If not, why? Or, think about your weekly, daily, or hourly meetings. For every hour of meeting time, what are the results? Do you see opportunities to establish specific meeting ground rules and processes that allow you to better capture the value of your people and teams?

As you think about each of these areas—hiring people, inspiring them, and managing teams, meetings, and conflicts—think about the traps that may be holding you back from realizing gains based on your efforts and investment. Is it the Expertise Trap, where people base solutions on previous experience, and avoid new approaches that might be more promising? The Winner's Trap, where people miss opportunities to learn and collaborate because they're too focused on individual incentives? Or have you fallen into the Agreement Trap, where people avoid voicing crucial information so that they can prevent contentious team dynamics? Are you struggling to help your people interact due to the Communication Trap, where they're overloaded with noise? Or do you see the signature of the Macromanagement Trap, where managers are waiting for employees to empower themselves and get things done—but it's just not happening?

The spending traps we've described here and advice we've given aren't meant to critique how managers work with their employees, clients, and superiors. Rather, they are intended to broaden managers' repertories of action and add a few new clubs to the golf bag. In fact, many of the managers we have worked with have the solutions at their fingertips, although they might not be readily obvious. These best practices include specific questions to ask, designs to implement, and experiments to test prospective solutions. Table 7-1 provides a recap of some of these practices—most of which shouldn't cost anything more than a thoughtful shift in perspective and planning.

TABLE 7-1

Spending traps and their solutions

Spending trap	Solutions to escape the trap
Expertise Trap	• Test your intuition by creating tests of disconfirmation. • Collect data from past experiences and analyze the reasons for success and failure. • Ask yourself different types of whys before creating a causal story. • Rather than fixating on specific solutions, use the problem-finding worksheet to gain a complete definition of the problem.
Winner's Trap	• Clarify the lines of cooperation and competition at work. • Get beyond financial incentives for performance and consider intangible resources that might be appealing. • Use the power of publicity to bring out people's social selves and better work. • Help winners become better quitters by emphasizing the gains from failure.
Agreement Trap	• Challenge the stereotypes about yourself. • Negotiate by aligning your argument with your priorities. • Explain why you're sharing a negative message in order to control people's processes of rationalization. • Get comfortable delivering the negative message rather than watering it down with compliments. • Encourage productive conflict.
Communication Trap	• Change your footpath at work to encourage random collisions between people. • Activate the diversity already present in your network. • Silence the noise with disciplined information search. • Unplug to create spaces where people can focus.
Macromanagement Trap	• Create ground rules and procedures for structured coordination. • Strike a balance between independent work and team collaboration. • Create the connective tissue between group members by talking through team processes and training people together. • Identify typical sequences of unproductive conflict and hijack them by developing new patterns of interaction.

Overcoming Obstacles

Still, we're well aware that the most challenging and wicked problems can't be put to rest with quick and easy solutions. Even with new strategies and the best of intentions, it's all too easy to face obstacles such as inertia and pushback and slip back into action without traction.

Tackling Inertia

As faculty who teach executive education courses, we've discovered that our executives' single largest desire out of classroom learning is that it translates into follow-through and lasting results. During our training sessions, most managers and leaders are highly energized, motivated, and downright resolute about changing their game. Then two things happen.

First, they return to their day-to-day organization and face a tidal wave of deliverables, requests for meetings, and hundreds of e-mails. The empowered feeling is wiped out almost instantaneously. The new ideas get trapped in the garbage can as other items rise to the top of the pile.

Or, because managers are often dealing with these people problems alone, they lack a community to back them up. More often than not, inertia takes hold and motivation fades, along with the detailed notes and action plans. The good intentions have no legs because there's no group to run with them.

In either case, the prospect of changing the way you work can be intimidating. But it does not have to be this way. To begin, pick one small piece of the puzzle to solve before diving in headfirst. If people don't know what to do, or are overwhelmed doing it, they fall off the wagon. Instead, choose one problem. Perhaps you're overwhelmed by the onslaught of communication in your inbox. Start by implementing a technology-free hour per week—just for you—and observe the result. If that helps restore your focus and productivity, expand the policy to the rest of your team. Or pick one thing to work on during the next meeting you lead. If you want to generate ideas, for example, choose a single session to experiment with brainwriting instead of brainstorming. You don't need to change everything at once to get some traction on the spending traps.

To simplify the change process further, revisit the chapter that you felt best described the traps in your organization as it is now. Identify one trap or one situation that you want to work through, and let that be your goal for this month.

Pushback from Your Team

As hard as it is to change your own approach, the challenges multiply as you introduce change to your employees. Your team members might initially find it awkward to create tests of disconfirmation or openly discuss negative information with a teammate (especially if that teammate is higher up in rank). They may be hesitant to jump into new ways of working that break their (and your) long-established habits. To encourage your team and get past the pushback, create clear-cut procedures and protocols with your team so that they have an investment in helping the new process succeed.

While you show your team confidence in a new way of working, also share with them when things aren't going as planned. As we mentioned in discussing the Winner's Trap, there's no stigma in failure. If you try a given tactic and it's not quite working for your team, be open about it, identify what's holding progress back, and adapt your approach.

These obstacles are particularly tractable because this book has deliberately avoided focusing on grand, overly ambitious changes. Instead, we've sought to identify fine-grained strategies that you can easily try and test with your team. By implementing a small change and helping it persist, it becomes a habit. In the words of Mahatma Gandhi:

Your beliefs become your thoughts,

Your thoughts become your words,

Your words become your actions,

Your actions become your habits,

Your habits become your values,

Your values become your destiny.[1]

What seems like a modest microchange can become a powerful new way of leading that transforms waste into value and meaningful impact.

———————

Let's return to Sandeep, who desperately wanted to fix the conflict and miscommunication on his team and finally solve the problems he was hired to handle. By walking through his process, we identify points where he resisted key traps, curbed the spending, and found workable solutions to the problems.

Sandeep's Journey

As you recall, Sandeep was a fast-thinking, accomplished manager with a demonstrated track record of excellence, and his team was full of high-level experts. His problem was clearly not a lack of talent or intellect, but he was still not getting the results he needed from his fractured group. There was competition within and between the functional groups, as team members vied for status and pushed for the development of over 150 new products. Sandeep realized that their demands were collectively unrealistic, but neither subgroup wanted to budge from their positions.

Sandeep's gut instinct was to persuade the team of where they were wrong—and he had already marshaled a long list of rational reasons to convince them that their plans were unworkable. In other words, he was racing headlong toward the spending traps.

Problem Finding

Sandeep was on the verge of barreling toward his definition of the problem and imposing it on everyone, but he recognized the Expertise Trap in play. Instead of leaning on his own habitual perception of what the problems were, he led a problem-finding discussion about the strategy. Sandeep listed all the functional areas and geographies, and asked each team member to identify the biggest issues, from the perspective of their functional group. He reminded them to steer away from proposing solutions, but instead, to summarize the key challenges.

To facilitate this discussion, Sandeep told everyone that their responses should be written in the form of questions, such as "How do we decrease the pipeline of products?" or "How do we collect data on which products are most effective?" After about thirty minutes, the team had posed more than forty questions. Sandeep then asked each functional group to sort the questions into piles—again, not focusing on solutions, but rather on how to define and organize the problems. Once the questions were sorted, Sandeep challenged the team as a whole to go one level deeper and study the relationship between the questions. Did one naturally come before another? Would solving one question help or thwart progress on another? During this time, Sandeep noticed that people (at least temporarily) stepped away from their own preferred solutions and were considering both the details and the big picture, the figure and the background.

Before long, the whole team had sketched out a framework of the potential problems. Like the blueprint for a house, they could now see which issues were foundational and which could be addressed only once those foundational problems were solved. They agreed on how the problems were organized and most important, instead of tearing down arguments, built and agreed upon a framework for moving forward!

The team concluded the discussion by identifying all the reasons why each of their patterns could be wrong—and developed a plan to collect the data that would allow them to determine whether they'd fixated on a signal or noise.

Assessing Options—Fairly and Openly

Sandeep knew that there were over one hundred potential new projects that the team could pursue—but they had no data to justify their prospects of success. And so, whenever there were conversations about which projects should live or die, the conversations were unproductive and contentious because they were based on gut feelings or the project champion's persistence—a key feature of the Winner's Trap. Sandeep understood why the meetings and conversations over the past year were going nowhere: they had essentially just created noise rather than meaningful signals. So, Sandeep challenged the team to develop a clear, unbiased methodology using empirical data and experimental approaches to test whether new projects would be viable. He referred to data from previous launches to see if there were any historical drivers of success that they could learn from to make sense of future launches.

Using that data, he plotted several projects on a spend-value matrix (figure 7-1), revealing the past investments in different projects. He then assessed the returns from that spending, staying true to the data and putting aside team members' feelings about the project. But he didn't simply employ a narrow financial calculation. He thought beyond the short-term financial value the investments had earned, and considered the broader returns in terms of relationships, time savings, and long-term benefits. He was able to study the most successful projects and understand some of the key drivers of

FIGURE 7-1

Spend-value matrix

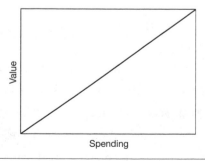

their successes. He also studied the failures and the underlying reasons why the team wasn't able to live up to its potential.

The data allowed him to lead a less emotional conversation about this subject with his team. They used the spend-value matrix to focus their discussion on the following three questions:

- Where are we getting commensurate value for our investment? (These items are plotted on the line.)

- Where are we spending and not receiving any value? (These items are plotted below the line.)

- Are there places where we spend very little and yet create value? (These items are plotted above the line.)

The conversation allowed the team to start to see some new opportunities as well as think about some places where hard choices might have to be made. The spend-value matrix revealed one particular project that was the pet idea of some of the most powerful players in the room. It was unlikely to yield the promised results and had to be carefully evaluated. Sandeep knew that the alphas were heavily invested in their baby. He also knew that the political nature of the discussion kept the rest of the group silent. At this point, the Winner's Trap and the Agreement Trap were still lurking in their discussions.

He pulled out his index cards again and asked his team to write where they saw the waste and value trade-offs. He cautioned them to maintain strict anonymity. He then collected all the cards so he could capture their insights.

Many had flagged the alphas' project as a laggard on the spend-value matrix. At this point, Sandeep raised the issue directly and escaped the Agreement Trap.

Sandeep needed to help the group raise the core issues dispassionately, not defensively. He decided to encourage some debate. He randomly assigned team members to argue either for or against this particular project, which meant that many of the alphas had to critique their baby honestly. By having this difficult conversation, the team was able to surface the serious concerns with the project.

The group decided to develop a clear protocol to evaluate the project's progress over the next three months, and Sandeep was able to lay the groundwork for its eventual termination if it wasn't meeting expectations. In the end, the team ended up using this methodology to evaluate all of the proposed projects.

Breaking Down Silos

Sandeep was relieved to get conversations about projects on the table and finally have his team members working with, not against, each other. But beyond the immediate problem, he wanted to get fresh ideas and perspectives for his team rather than falling into a Communication Trap. He organized a "lunch and learn," bringing in a diverse cross-section of people from throughout the organization: different geographical areas, different statuses, and different functional areas.

Instead of allowing the group to break bread in their usual cliques, however, Sandeep assigned the seating to split up the coalitions. At first, this disgruntled some. Several people muttered, "Since when do we have assigned seating?" and one even sarcastically remarked, "This feels like my daughter's fifth-grade class." But before long, people were deep in conversation with others they'd never have chosen to sit by on their own.

The group then turned to the "learn" part of the event. Sandeep and his team took notes on what their colleagues throughout the firm had learned in their own processes. Naturally, some of their ideas wouldn't be workable on Sandeep's team. But Sandeep wrote down five new and potentially promising ideas that his team had never thought about in all their hours together in the echo chamber.

Moving forward, Sandeep didn't want to lose this infusion of new perspectives. He regularly invited outsiders to his team and assigned smaller multifunctional teams for future projects and discussions.

Keeping the Momentum Going

Sandeep had created that buzz and energy within his team that every leader hopes for. It wasn't all warm and fuzzy—they also broached some contentious issues, but they did so in a way that didn't lead to a predictable conflict spiral. There were moments when Sandeep was able to create inspiring opportunities that allowed the team to see their chance to be industry leaders. He felt that people were beginning to view each other not as competitors in a zero-sum game, but as partners who could help create an expanding pie.

Rather than loosening the reins at this point and falling into the Macromanagement Trap, Sandeep realized that the momentary burst of inspiration from these exercises and conversations wouldn't necessarily translate into meaningful behavioral changes. He might have created some potential value, but the real challenge would be implementing and capturing that value over the long term. To coordinate the group's execution of the strategy, Sandeep gave the group three key "starter" questions to help them chart their group process:

- What is our mission?

- What are the norms by which we work?

- What role does each person play?

However, Sandeep quickly realized how uncomfortable his group was with introspection. So he asked each person to respond by writing their answers to these questions anonymously on cards. He led the group through each of these questions to establish some clear ground rules for their work.

In addition to discussing the high-level mission, the group also drilled down to map out its specific goals moving forward. Although the problem-finding exercise they had done earlier had surfaced several critical issues, they decided to pick only a few high-priority items to focus on so that they wouldn't get overwhelmed and lose traction. They developed a road map of milestones for each of those and measurable outputs at each milestone.

They also defined the process by which they could best work together over the next six months. They marked off several rapid check-ins at key decision points so that the process simulated a cave and commons. And to create the necessary connective tissue, they defined each member's strengths and interests so that they could contribute their critical expertise. Sandeep looked at the calendar and chose a date when each of the team members would report what they accomplished.

Sandeep didn't know if he'd successfully tamed the wicked problems that had stymied his team and could declare victory. But he did know that he didn't just see people problems, but rather viewed his people as the principle resource for solving them.

Conclusion

As wicked as people problems can be, they don't need to become persistent spending traps. The guidelines and best practices in this book focus on developing mental models based on signals rather than noise so you can regain the connection between your managerial actions and their consequences. When you stop spending and start managing, this doesn't just save your organization money, it also saves you—and your employees—time, energy, and frustration as you get traction on your hardest problems. And you may just discover new value in yourself and your people that has been hidden this whole time.

Notes

Chapter 1

1. All of the names and companies in this book are heavily disguised composites.

2. Of these executives, 60 percent were American, 32 percent Asian, 5 percent European, and the rest were from other regions. They represented a cross-section of industries (17 percent public administration, 26 percent services, 12 percent finance, insurance, and real estate, 7 percent retail and wholesale trade, 6 percent transportation and utilities, 19 percent manufacturing, 7 percent construction, 6 percent agriculture, mining, forestry) and functional areas (5 percent finance, 11 percent marketing, 22 percent operations, 25 percent general management, 10 percent sales, 2 percent human resources, 25 percent other).

3. Numbers total to over 100 percent because executives could check all that were relevant if their company used multiple approaches.

4. C.W. Churchman, "Wicked Problems," *Management Science* 14, no. 4 (1967): B141–B146.

5. H.W.J. Rittel and M.W. Weber, "Dilemmas in a General Theory of Planning," *Policy Science* 4 (1973): 155–169. See also John C. Camillus's excellent article on wicked problems in strategy formulation for these and other criteria in defining wicked problems, "Strategy as a Wicked Problem," *Harvard Business Review* (May 2008).

6. These insights about the varied types of costs emerged in our executives' essays.

7. N. Clark, "The Airbus Saga: Crossed Wires and a Multibillion-Euro Delay," *New York Times*, December 11, 2006.

8. Ibid.

9. J. Lawler, "The Real Cost of Workplace Conflict," *Entrepreneur*, June 21, 2010, http://www.entrepreneur.com/article/207196.

10. See also Christine Pearson and Christine Porath's book, *The Cost of Bad Behavior: How Incivility Is Damaging Your Business and What to Do About It* (New York: Portfolio, 2009).

11. For a thoughtful analysis of how to quantify the intangibles in business, see Douglas W. Hubbard, *How to Measure Anything* (New York: Wiley, 2014).

12. M.D. Cohen, J.G. March, and J.P. Olsen, "A Garbage Can Model of Organizational Choice," *Administrative Science Quarterly* 17, no. 1 (1972): 1–25.

13. W. Kempton, "Two Theories of Home Heat Control," *Cognitive Science* 10 (1986): 75–90.

14. L.W. Nelson and J.W. MacArthur, "Energy Savings Through Thermostat Setbacks," *ASHRE Transactions* 83, no. 1 (1978): 319–333.

15. D.A. Levinthal and J.G. March, "The Myopia of Learning," *Strategic Management Journal* 14 (1993): 95–112.

16. D. Kahneman and S. Frederick, "Representativeness Revisited: Attribute Substitution in Intuitive Judgment," in *Heuristics and Biases: The Psychology of Intuitive Judgment*, ed. T. Gilovich, D. Griffin, and D. Kahneman (New York: Cambridge University Press, 2002), 49–81.

17. Strategy professor Michael Leiblein offers this example.

18. B. Schneier, "Changing Passwords," *Schneier on Security* (blog), November 11, 2010, http://schneier.com/blog/archives/2010/11/changing_passwo.html.

19. W.G. Chase and H.A. Simon, "Perception in Chess," *Cognitive Psychology* 4 (1973): 55–81.

20. B. Wansink, J.E. Painter, and J. North, "Why Visual Cues of Portion Size May Influence Intake," *Obesity Research* 13, no. 1 (2005): 93–100.

21. J.W. Getzels, "Problem Finding: A Theoretical Note," *Cognitive Science* 3, no. 2 (1979): 167–172.

22. J.A. Goncalo and B.M. Staw, "Individualism-Collectivism and Group Creativity," *Organizational Behavior and Human Decision Processes* 100 (2006): 96–109.

23. T. Menon and L. Thompson, "Don't Hate Me Because I'm Beautiful: Self-Enhancing Biases in Threat Appraisal," *Organizational Behavior and Human Decision Processes* 104, no. 1 (2007): 45–60.

24. A. Edmondson, "Speaking Up in the Operating Room: How Team Leaders Promote Learning in Interdisciplinary Action Teams," *Journal of Management Studies* 40, no. 6 (2003): 1419–1452.

25. K.W. Phillips and D.L. Loyd, "When Surface and Deep-Level Diversity Collide: The Effects on Dissenting Group Members," *Organizational Behavior and Human Decision Processes* 99, no. 2 (2006): 143–160.

26. J. Pfeffer and R.I. Sutton, "The Smart Talk Trap," *Harvard Business Review* (May 1999).

27. M. McPherson, L. Smith-Lovin, and M. Brashears, "The Ties That Bind Are Fraying," *Contexts* 7, no. 3 (2008): 32–36.

28. N. Atkin, "40% of Staff Time Is Wasted on Reading Internal Emails," *The Guardian*, December 17, 2012, http://www.theguardian.com/housing-network/2012/dec/17/ban-staff-email-halton-housing-trust.

29. J. Goldenberg and M. Levy, "Distance Is Not Dead: Social Interaction and Geographical Distance in the Internet Era," *Computers and Society* 2 (2009): 1–22.

30. K. Lewin, R. Lippitt, and R.K. White, "Patterns of aggressive behavior in experimentally created 'social climates,'" *Journal of Social Psychology* 10 (1939): 271–299.

31. L. Thompson and T.R. Cohen, "Metacognition in Teams and Organizations," in *Social Metacognition: Frontiers of Social Psychology*, ed. P. Brinol and K. DeMarree (New York: Psychology Press, 2012).

32. R.L. Moreland, L. Argote, and R. Krishnan, "Training People to Work in Groups," in *Theory and Research on Small Groups*, ed. R.S. Tindale et al. (New York: Plenum Press, 1998).

Chapter 2

1. H. Simon, "A Behavioral Model of Rational Choice," *Quarterly Journal of Economics* 69 (1955): 99–118.

2. M. Winter, "Timeline Details Missteps with Ebola Patient Who Died," *USA Today*, October 18, 2014, http://www.usatoday.com/story/news/nation/2014/10/17/ebola-duncan-congress-timeline/17456825/.

3. J.W. Getzels, "Problem Finding: A Theoretical Note," *Cognitive Science* 3, no. 2 (1979): 167–172.

4. J.A.Whitson and A.D. Galinsky, "Lacking Control Increases Illusory Pattern Perception," *Science* 322, no. 5898 (2008): 115–117.

5. C. Wang, J. Whitson, and T. Menon, "Culture and Pattern Perception: American and East Asian Faith in Horoscopes," *Social Psychological and Personality Science* 3 (2012): 630–638.

6. The character 骂 (mà) comprises the radical for "mother" on the bottom, with the two squares above representing the radical for mouth.

7. L. Rivera, *Pedigree: How Elite Students Get Elite Jobs* (Princeton, NJ: Princeton University Press, 2015).

8. J. Sundberg, "What Is the True Cost of Hiring a Bad Employee?" *Undercover Recruiter*, http://theundercoverrecruiter.com/infographic-what-cost-hiring-wrong-employee/.

9. J. Pfeffer and R.I. Sutton, "Evidence-Based Management," *Harvard Business Review*, January 2006, https://hbr.org/2006/01/evidence-based-management.

10. P. Wason, "On the Failure to Eliminate Hypotheses in a Conceptual Task," *Quarterly Journal of Experimental Psychology* 12, no. 3 (1960): 129–140.

11. R.S. Nickerson, "Confirmation Bias: A Ubiquitous Phenomenon in Many Guises," *Review of General Psychology* 2, no. 2 (June 1998): 175–200.

12. M. Snyder, E.D. Tanke, and E. Berscheid, "Social Perception and Interpersonal Behavior: On the Self-Fulfilling Nature of Social Stereotypes," *Journal of Experimental Social Psychology* 35 (1977): 656–666.

13. M. Snyder and W.B. Swann Jr., "Hypothesis Testing Processes in Social Interaction," *Journal of Personality and Social Psychology* 36 (1978): 1202–1212.

14. I. Bohnet, A. van Geen, M. Bazerman, "When Performance Trumps Gender Bias: Joint versus Separate Evaluation," *Management Science* (forthcoming).

15. C. Goldin and C. Rouse, "Orchestrating Impartiality: The Impact of 'Blind' Auditions on Female Musicians," *American Economic Review* 90, no. 4 (2000): 715–741.

16. J. Dana, R.M. Dawes, and N. Peterson, "Belief in the Unstructured Interview: The Persistence of an Illusion," *Judgment and Decision Making* 8 (2013): 512–520.

17. J. Pfeffer and R.I. Sutton, "The Smart-Talk Trap," *Harvard Business Review*, May–June 1999.

18. R. Dawes, "The Robust Beauty of Improper Linear Models in Decision Making," *American Psychologist* 34 (1979): 571–582.

19. A. Pluchino, C. Garofalo, A. Rapisarda, S.Spagano, and M. Caserta, "Accidental Politicians: How Randomly Selected Legislators Can Improve Parliament Efficiency," *Physica A* 390, nos. 21–22 (October 2011): 3944–3954.

20. M. Morris and K. Peng, "Culture and Cause: American and Chinese Attributions for Social and Physical Events," *Journal of Personality and Social Psychology* 67, no. 6 (1994): 949–971.

21. T. Menon et al., "Blazing the Trail versus Trailing the Group: Culture and Perceptions of the Leader's Position," *Organizational Behavior and Human Decision Processes* 113 (2010): 551–561.

22. T. Masuda et al., "Culture and Aesthetic Preference: Comparing the Attention to Context of East Asians and Americans," *Personality and Social Psychology Bulletin* 34, no. 9 (2008): 1260–1275.

23. L. Ross, "The Intuitive Psychologist and His Shortcomings: Distortions in the Attribution Process," in *Advances in Experimental Social Psychology*, vol. 10, ed. L. Berkowitz (Orlando, FL: Academic Press, 1977), 173–220.

24. H.H. Kelley and J.L. Michela, "Attribution Theory and Research, *Annual Review of Psychology* 31, no. 1 (1980): 457–501.

25. B. Weiner, *An Attributional Theory of Motivation and Emotion* (New York: Springer, 1986).

26. R.J. Klimaski and R.A. Ash, "Accountability and Negotiation Behavior," *Organizational Behavior and Human Performance* 11, no. 3 (1974): 409–425.

27. T. Menon et al., "Culture and the Construal of Agency: Attribution to Individual versus Group Dispositions," *Journal of Personality and Social Psychology* 76 (1999): 701–717.

28. UNICEF, *Fact Sheet: Malaria, A Global Crisis*, August 27, 2004, www.unicef.org/media/media_20475.html.

29. L. Macinnis, "Preventing Malaria Deaths to Cost $5 Billion a Year," *Reuters*, September 25, 2008, http://www.reuters.com/article/us-malaria-deaths-idUSTRE48O82820080925.

30. "Malaria-Fighting 'Faso Soap' Wins Global Social Venture Competition Grand Prize, People's Choice Award," http://blumcenter.berkeley.edu/news-posts/faso-soap/.

31. K. Duncker, "On Problem Solving," *Psychological Monographs* 58, no. 5 (1945): i–113.

32. D.H. Clements, "Teaching and Learning Geometry," in *Research Companion to Principles and Standards for School Mathematics*, ed. J. Kilpatrick, W.G. Martin, and D. Schifter (Reston, VA: National Council of Teachers of Mathematics, 2003), 151–178.

Chapter 3

1. B. Keim, "Taking Traffic Control Lessons—from Ants," *Wired*, 2009, http://www.wired.com/2009/02/anttraffic/.

2. Associated Press, "Study: Self-Driving Cars Would Eliminate Majority of Traffic Deaths, Congestion," October 23, 2013, http://washington.cbslocal.com/2013/10/23/study-self-driving-cars-would-eliminate-majority-of-traffic-deaths-congestion.

3. J.A. Goncalo and B.M. Staw, "Individualism-Collectivism and Group Creativity," *Organizational Behavior and Human Decision Processes* 100 (2006): 96–109.

4. T. Menon and S. Blount, "The Messenger Bias: A Relational Model of Knowledge Variation," *Research in Organizational Behavior* 25 (2003): 137–186.

5. T. Menon and J. Pfeffer, "Valuing Internal versus External Knowledge: Explaining the Preference for Outsiders," *Management Science* 49 (2003): 497–513.

6. T. Menon, L. Thompson, and H. Choi, "Tainted Knowledge versus Tempting Knowledge: Why People Avoid Knowledge from Internal Rivals and Seek Knowledge from External Rivals," *Management Science* 52 (2006): 1129–1144.

7. T. Menon, O.J. Sheldon, and A.D. Galinsky, "Barriers to Transforming Hostile Relations: Why Friendly Gestures Can Backfire," *Negotiation and Conflict Management Research* 7 (2014): 17–37.

8. See Adam Galinsky and Maurice Schweitzer's excellent book *Friend and Foe* (New York: Crown Business, 2015) on navigating competitive and cooperative situations.

9. Menon and Pfeffer, "Valuing Internal versus External Knowledge."

10. S. Kerr, "On the Folly of Rewarding A, While Hoping for B," *Academy of Management Executive* 9, no. 1 (1995): 7–14.

11. http://profootballtalk.nbcsports.com/2010/11/09/ terrell-owens-on-pace-to-reach-every-contract-incentive/.

12. T. Gibson, "How NFL Contracts Are Helping NFL Players but Hurting Their Teams," *Washington Post*, January 15, 2014, https:// www.washingtonpost.com/news/monkey-cage/wp/2014/01/15/ how-nfl-contracts-are-helping-nfl-players-but-hurting-their-teams/.

13. T. Menon and L. Thompson, "Envy at Work," *Harvard Business Review*, April 2010.

14. K. Hedges, "If You Think Leadership Development Is a Waste of Time, You May Be Right," *Forbes*, September 23, 2014, http://www .forbes.com/sites/work-in-progress/2014/09/23/if-you-think-leadership-development-is-a-waste-of-time-you-may-be-right/#660a3b8c5dcc.

15. T. Davenport and L. Prusak, "Know What You Know," *CIO*, March 26, 1998.

16. G.J. Kilduff, H.A. Elfenbein, and B.M. Staw, "The Psychology of Rivalry: A Relationally-Dependent Analysis of Competition," *Academy of Management Journal* 53 (2010): 943–969.

17. M.K. Duffy et al., "A Social Context Model of Envy and Social Undermining," *Academy of Management Journal* 55, no. 3 (2012): 643–666.

18. A. Tesser, "Toward a Self-Evaluation Maintenance Model of Social Behavior," *Advances in Experimental Social Psychology* 21 (1988): 181–227.

19. C.M. Steele, "The Psychology of Self-Affirmation: Sustaining the Integrity of the Self," *Advances in Experimental Social Psychology* 21 (1988): 261–302.

20. Menon, Thompson, and Choi, "Tainted Knowledge versus Tempting Knowledge."

21. C. Heath, "On the Social Psychology of Agency Relationships: Lay Theories of Motivation Over-Emphasize Extrinsic Rewards," *Organizational Behavior and Human Decision Processes* 78, no. 1 (1999), 25–62.

22. Uriel and Edna Foa developed this framework (U.G. Foa and E.B. Foa, *Society Structures of the Mind* [Springfield: Thomas, 1974]), and Cohen and Bradford developed an even broader set of hidden resources beyond money "your currencies of exchange" (A.R. Cohen and D.L.

Bradford, *Influence without Authority* [New Jersey: Wiley & Sons, 2005]).

23. Ibid.

24. Ibid.

25. K.D. Vohs, N.L. Mead, and M.R. Goode, "The Psychological Consequences of Money," *Science* 314, no. 5802 (2006): 1154–1156.

26. S.E. DeVoe and J. House, "Time, Money, and Happiness: How Does Putting a Price on Time Affect Our Ability to Smell the Roses?" *Journal of Experimental Social Psychology* 48, no. 2 (2012): 466–474.

27. S.E. DeVoe and J. Pfeffer. "The Stingy Hour: How Accounting for Time Affects Volunteering," *Personality and Social Psychology Bulletin* 36, no. 4 (2009): 470–483.

28. J. Porter, "Observations from a Tipless Restaurant, Part 1: Overview," *Jay Porter* (blog), July 25, 2013, jayporter.com/dispatches/observations-from-a-tipless-restaurant-part-1-overview/.

29. A.M. Grant, "Does Intrinsic Motivation Fuel the Prosocial Fire? Motivational Synergy in Predicting Persistence, Performance, and Productivity," *Journal of Applied Psychology* 93, no. 1 (2008): 48–56.

30. G. Loewenstein, L. Thompson, and M. Bazerman, "Social Utility and Decision Making in Interpersonal Contexts," *Journal of Personality and Social Psychology* 57 (1989): 426–441.

31. D.M. Messick and K.P. Sentis, "Fairness and Preference," *Journal of Experimental Social Psychology* 15 (1979): 418–434.

32. M. Ross and F. Sicoly, "Egocentric Biases in Availability and Attribution," *Journal of Personality and Social Psychology* 37 (1979): 322–336.

33. D.M. Rousseau, "Psychological and Implied Contracts in Organizations," *Employee Responsibilities and Rights Journal* 2 (1989): 121–139.

34. C. Shea and T. Menon, "How Networks Make Liars and Liars Make Networks: Reciprocal Causation between Ethical Norm Violation and Network Activation" (working paper, The Ohio State University Fisher College of Business, 2016).

35. E. Miron-Spektor et al., "Others' Anger Makes People Work Harder Not Smarter: The Effect of Observing Anger and Sarcasm on Creative and Analytic Thinking," *Journal of Applied Psychology* 96, no. 5 (2011): 1065–1075.

36. J. Haidt, *The Righteous Mind: Why Good People Are Divided by Politics and Religion* (New York: Pantheon, 2012).

37. D. Chowdhury, K. Nishinari, and N. Schadschneider, "Self-Organized Patterns and Traffic Flow in Colonies of Organisms: From Bacteria and Social Insects to Vertebrates," *Phase Transitions* 77 (2004): 601–624.

38. B.M. Staw, "Knee-Deep in the Big Muddy: A Study of Escalating Commitment to a Chosen Course of Action," *Organizational Behavior and Human Performance* 16, no. 1 (1976): 27–44.

39. Ibid.

40. H. Takeuchi and I. Nonaka, "The New New Product Development Game," *Harvard Business Review* (January 1986): 285–305.

41. K. Schwaber and J. Sutherland, *Software in 30 Days: How Agile Managers Beat the Odds, Delight Their Customers, and Leave Competitors in the Dust* (Hoboken, NJ: Wiley, 2012).

42. This example is drawn from http://www.dvorak.org/blog/whatever -happened-to-the-ibm-stretch-computer/.

43. R.L. Dillon and C.H. Tinsley, "How Near-Misses Influence Decision Making under Risk: A Missed Opportunity for Learning," *Management Science* 54, no. 8 (2008): 1425–1440.

Chapter 4

1. "Doctor Who Cut Off Wrong Leg Is Defended by Colleagues," *New York Times*, September 17, 1995, http://www.nytimes.com/1995/09/17/us/ doctor-who-cut-off-wrong-leg-is-defended-by-colleagues.html; A. Jauregui, "Man Gets Accidental Vasectomy after Doctors Operate on 'Wrong Site,'" *Huffington Post*, May 6, 2014, http://www.huffingtonpost .com/2014/05/06/accidental-vasectomy-wrong-site_n_5273865.html.

2. S.G. Boodman, "The Pain of Wrong Site Surgery," *Washington Post*, June 20, 2011, https://www.washingtonpost.com/national/the-pain-of- wrong-site-surgery/2011/06/07/AGK3uLdH_story.html.

3. "Trail of Errors Led to 3 Wrong Brain Surgeries," *NBC News*, December 14, 2007, nbcnews.com, http://www.nbcnews.com/id/22263412/ ns/health-health_care/t/trail-errors-led-wrong-brain-surgeries/.

4. Boodman, "The Pain of Wrong Site Surgery."

5. E.W. Morrison and F.J. Milliken, "Organizational Silence: A Barrier to Change and Development in a Pluralistic World," *Academy of Management Review* 25, no. 4 (2000): 706–725.

6. R. Merkel, "Where Were the Whistleblowers in the Volkswagen Emissions Scandal?" *The Conversation*, September 29, 2015, http:// theconversation.com/where-were-the-whistleblowers-in-the-volkswagen- emissions-scandal-48249.

7. J. Plungis and D. Hull, "VW's Emissions Cheating Found by Clean-Air Group," *Bloomberg Business*, September 19, 2015, http://www.bloomberg.com/news/articles/2015-09-19/ volkswagen-emissions-cheating-found-by-curious-clean-air-group.

8. T. Higgins and N. Summers, "GM Recalls: How General Motors Silenced a Whistle-Blower," *Bloomberg Business*, June

18, 2014, http://www.bloomberg.com/bw/articles/2014-06-18/
gm-recalls-whistle-blower-was-ignored-mary-barra-faces-congress.

9. "GM Agrees $900m Settlement for Faulty Ignition Switches," *BBC*,
September 17, 2015, http://www.bbc.com/news/business-34276419.

10. F.J. Milliken and E.W. Morrison, "Shades of Silence:
Emerging Themes and Future Directions for Research on Silence in
Organizations," *Journal of Management Studies* 40, no. 6 (2003):
1563–1568.

11. C.K.W. De Dreu and L.R. Weingart, "Task versus Relationship
Conflict, Team Performance, and Team Member Satisfaction: A Meta-
Analysis," *Journal of Applied Psychology* 88, no. 4 (2003): 741–749.

12. D.M. Rousseau, "Psychological and Implied Contracts in
Organizations," *Employee Responsibilities and Rights Journal* 2 (1989):
121–139.

13. Milliken and Morrison, "Shades of Silence."

14. J.R. Detert and A.C. Edmondson. "Implicit Voice Theories: Taken-
for-Granted Rules of Self-Censorship at Work," *Academy of Management
Journal* 54, no. 3 (June 2011): 461–488.

15. K.D. Harber, R. Stafford, and K. Kennedy, "The Positive Feedback
Bias as a Response to Self-Image Threat," *British Journal of Social
Psychology* (in press).

16. De Dreu and Weingart, "Task versus Relationship Conflict, Team
Performance, and Team Member Satisfaction."

17. C. Whelan, "Why Smart Men Marry Smart Women," (excerpt) *ABC
News*, 2006, http://abcnews.go.com/GMA/Books/story?id=2569852&page=1.

18. Ibid.

19. S. Shippy, "Why Do People Who Went to Harvard Sometimes Say
'I Went to School in Boston' When Asked Where They Went to College?"
[Quora.com forum comment]. September 10, 2010, https://www.quora
.com/Why-do-people-who-went-to-Harvard-sometimes-say-I-went-to-
school-in-Boston-when-asked-where-they-went-to-college.

20. T. Menon and L. Thompson, "Don't Hate Me Because I'm Beautiful:
Self-Enhancing Biases in Threat Appraisal," *Organizational Behavior and
Human Decision Processes* 104, no. 1 (2007): 45–60.

21. E.T. Amanatullah, M.W. Morris, and J.R. Curhan, "Negotiators
Who Give Too Much: Unmitigated Communion, Relational Anxieties, and
Economic Costs in Distributive and Integrative Bargaining," *Journal of
Personality and Social Psychology* 95, no. 3 (2008): 723–738.

22. Menon and Thompson, "Don't Hate Me Because I'm Beautiful."

23. A. Kalev, F. Dobbin, and E. Kelly, "Best Practices or Best Guesses?
Assessing the Efficacy of Corporate Affirmative Action and Diversity
Policies," *American Sociological Review* 71 (2006): 589–617.

24. E. Apfelbaum, S.E. Sommers, and M.I. Norton, "Seeing Race and Seeming Racist? Evaluating Strategic Colorblindness in Social Interaction," *Journal of Personality and Social Psychology* 95, no. 4 (2008): 918–932.

25. V.C. Plaut and H.R. Markus, *Basically We're All The Same? Models of Diversity and the Dilemma of Difference* (unpublished manuscript, University California, Berkeley, 2007).

26. J.R. Curhan, "Why It Pays to Build Relationships," Program on Negotiation at Harvard Law School, September 6, 2011, http://www.pon.harvard.edu/daily/why-it-pays-to-build-relationships/.

27. W.R. Fry, I.J. Firestone, and D.L. Williams, "Negotiation Process and Outcome of Stranger Dyads and Dating Couples: Do Lovers Lose?" *Basic and Applied Social Psychology* 4, no. 1 (1983): 1–16.

28. J.R. Curhan et al., "Relational Accommodation in Negotiation: Effects of Egalitarianism and Gender on Economic Efficiency and Relational Capital," *Organizational Behavior and Human Decision Processes* 107 (2008): 192–205.

29. R.M. Krauss and S.R. Fussell, "Social Psychological Models of Interpersonal Communication," in *Social Psychology: A Handbook of Basic Principles*, ed. E.T. Higging and A. Kruglanski (New York: Guilford, 2006), 655–701.

30. K.L. McGinn, "Relationships and Negotiations in Context," in *Frontiers of Social Psychology: Negotiation Theory and Research*, ed. L. Thompson (New York: Psychological Press, 2006), 129–144.

31. U. Gneezy, K.L. Leonard, and J.A. List, "Gender Differences in Competition: Evidence from a Matrilineal and a Patriarchal Society," *Econometrica* (2009): 1637–1664.

32. T.A. Judge, B.A. Livingston, and C. Hurst, "Do Nice Guys—and Gals—Really Finish Last? The Joint Effects of Sex and Agreeableness on Income," *Journal of Personality and Social Psychology*, 102 (2012): 390–407.

33. L. Babcock et al., "Nice Girls Don't Ask," *Harvard Business Review*, October 2003.

34. F.J. Flynn, "What Have You Done For Me Lately? Temporal Adjustments To Favor Evaluations," *Organizational Behavior and Human Decision Processes* 91, no. 1 (2003): 38–50.

35. L.J. Kray and A.D. Galinsky, "Reversing the Gender Gap in Negotiations: An Exploration of Stereotype Regeneration," *Organizational Behavior and Human Decision Processes* 87 (2002): 386–410.

36. H.R. Bowles, L. Babcock, and K.L. McGinn, "Constraints and Triggers: Situational Mechanics of Gender in Negotiation," *Journal of Personality and Social Psychology* 89 (2005): 951–965.

37. R. Fisher and W. Ury, *Getting to Yes: Negotiating Agreement without Giving In* (Boston: Houghton Mifflin, 1992).

38. A.D. Galinsky et al., "Why It Pays to Get Inside the Head of Your Opponent: The Differential Effects of Perspective Taking and Empathy in Negotiations," *Psychological Science* 19, no. 4 (2008): 378–384.

39. R. Gagliano, "Gloria Steinem's Guide to Maneuvering around Misogyny," The Dinner Party Download, November 6, 2015, http://www .dinnerpartydownload.org/gloria-steinem/.

40. L. Thompson, "Information Exchange in Negotiation," *Journal of Experimental Social Psychology* 27, no. 2 (1991): 161–179.

41. V.H. Medvec and A.D. Galinsky, "Putting More on the Table: How Making Multiple Offers Can Increase the Final Value of the Deal," *Harvard Business School Negotiation Newsletter*, April 2005.

42. L. Thompson, "Information Exchange in Negotiation," *Journal of Experimental Social Psychology* 27, no. 2 (1991): 161–179.

43. A.L. Becker, "Checklists, Teamwork Minimizing Mistakes in Medicine," *The CT Mirror*, May 28, 2012, http://ctmirror.org/2012/05/28/ checklists-teamwork-minimizing-mistakes-medicine/.

44. Ibid.

45. "Quality-in-Action at Mayo Clinic," *Mayo Magazine* (Spring 2008), http://www.mayoclinic.org/documents/mc2386-sp08-pdf/doc-20078987.

46. R.B. Cialdini, *Influence: The Psychology of Persuasion*, rev. ed. (New York: Harper Business, 2006).

47. V.S. Folkes, "Recent Attribution Research in Consumer Behavior: A Review and New Directions," *Journal of Consumer Research* 14, no. 4 (1988): 548–565; J.J. Skowronski and D.E. Carlson, "Negativity and Extremity Biases in Impression Formation: A Review of Explanations," *Psychological Bulletin* 109 (1989): 131–142.

48. K.W. Phillips, "How Diversity Makes Us Smarter," *Scientific American*, September 16, 2014, http://www.scientificamerican.com/article/ how-diversity-makes-us-smarter/.

49. P. Koch, B. Koch, T. Menon, and O. Shenkar, "Complementary vs. Conflicting: Cultural Friction in Leadership Beliefs and Chinese Joint Venture Survival," *Journal of International Business Studies*, forthcoming.

50. M. Roberto, "Cutting Your Losses: How to Avoid the Sunk Cost Trap," *Ivey Business Journal*, 2009, http://iveybusinessjournal.com/ publication/cutting-your-losses-how-to-avoid-the-sunk-cost-trap/.

Chapter 5

1. G.M. Klump and H.C. Gerhardt, "Mechanisms and Function of Call-Timing in Male-Male Interactions in Frogs," in *Playback and Studies of Animal Communication*, ed. P.K. McGregor (New York: Plenum, 1992), 153–174.

2. R.H. Wiley, "Signal Detection and Animal Communication," *Advances in the Study of Behavior* 36 (2006): 217–247.

3. M.D. Cohen, J.G. March, and J.P. Olsen, "A Garbage Can Model of Organizational Choice," *Administrative Science Quarterly* 17, no. 1 (1972): 1–25.

4. N. Burg, "How Technology Has Changed Workplace Communication," *Forbes*, December 10, 2013, http://www.forbes.com/sites/unify/2013/12/10/how-technology-has-changed-workplace-communication/#503aecda4562.

5. J. Manyika, M. Chui, and H. Sarrazin, "Social Media's Productivity Payoff," *Harvard Business Review*, August 21, 2012, https://hbr.org/2012/08/social-medias-productivity-pay/.

6. K. Elsbach and D. Cable, "Why Showing Your Face at Work Matters," *Sloan Management Review*, June 19, 2012, http://sloanreview.mit.edu/article/why-showing-your-face-at-work-matters/; T.L. Dumas, K.W. Phillips, and N.P. Rothbard, "Getting Closer at the Company Party: Integration Experiences, Racial Dissimilarity and Workplace Relationships," *Organization Science* 24 (2013): 1377–1401.

7. M.L. Diamond, "What's the Biggest Distraction at Work? Co-Workers," *Asbury Park Press*, July 10, 2014, http://www.app.com/story/money/business/inthemoney/2014/07/10/whats-the-biggest-distraction-at-work-co-workers/12473573/.

8. M.S. Granovetter, "The Strength of Weak Ties," *American Journal of Sociology* 78 (1973): 1360–1380.

9. R.S. Burt, *Structural Holes: The Social Structure of Competition* (Cambridge, MA: Harvard University Press, 1992).

10. E.B. Smith, T. Menon, and L. Thompson, "High and Low Status Groups Activate Different Network Structures Under Job Threat," *Organization Science* 23 (2012): 67–82.

11. Burt, *Structural Holes*.

12. R.S. Burt, *Brokerage and Closure* (New York: Oxford University Press, 2005).

13. M. Grandjean, "Social network analysis and visualization: Moreno's Sociograms revisited," Martin Grandjean blog, March 16, 2015, http://www.martingrandjean.ch/social-network-analysis-visualization-morenos-sociograms-revisited/.

14. J.L. Moreno, *Who Shall Survive? A New Approach to the Problem of Human Interrelations* (Washington, DC: Nervous and Mental Disease Publishing Company, 1934); cited in L.C. Freeman, "Visualizing Social Networks," *Journal of Social Sciences* 1 (2000): 4, http://www.cmu.edu/joss/content/articles/volume1/Freeman.html.

15. Adapted from J. Cook, "Cosponsorship Networks in the U.S. Senate as of March 1, 2009," *Irregular Times*, http://irregulartimes.com/2009/03/01/cosponsorship-networks-in-the-us-senate-as-of-march-1-2009.

16. G. Tett, "*The Silo Effect: The Peril of Expertise and the Promise of Breaking Down Barriers* (New York: Simon and Schuster, 2015).

17. R.S. Burt, "Structural Holes and Good Ideas," *American Journal of Sociology* 110, no. 2 (2004): 349–399.

18. Ibid.

19. Ibid.

20. R.S. Burt, *Neighbor Networks: Competitive Advantage Local and Personal* (New York: Oxford University Press, 2009).

21. B. Uzzi and S. Dunlap, "How to Build Your Network," *Harvard Business Review* (December 2005): 53–60.

22. D. Marmaros and B. Sacerdote, "How Do Friendships Form?" *The Quarterly Journal of Economics* 121, no. 1 (2006): 79–119.

23. "Visualizing Friendships: The World According to Facebook," *Fox News*, December 14, 2010, http://www.foxnews.com/tech/2010/12/14/visualizing-friendships-world-according-facebook.html.

24. A. Chakravarti, T. Menon, and C. Winship, "Contact and Group Structure: A Natural Experiment of Interracial College Roommate Groups," *Organizational Science* 25, no. 4 (2014): 1216–1233.

25. A. Pentland, "The New Science of Building Great Teams," *Harvard Business Review*, April 2012, https://hbr.org/2012/04/the-new-science-of-building-great-teams.

26. H-S. Choi and L. Thompson," Old Wine in a New Bottle: Impact of Membership Change on Group Creativity," *Organizational Behavior and Human Decision Processes* 98, no. 2 (2005): 121–132.

27. R.B. Lount and K.W. Phillips, "Working Harder with the Out-Group: The Impact of Social Category Diversity on Motivation Gains," *Organizational Behavior and Human Decision Processes* 103, no. 2 (2007): 214–224.

28. E.B. Smith, T. Menon, and L. Thompson, "High and Low Status Groups Activate Different Network Structures Under Job Threat," *Organization Science* 23 (2012): 67–82.

29. C. Shea et al., "The Affective Antecedents of Cognitive Network Activation," *Social Networks* 43 (2015): 91–99.

30. D. Gigone and R. Hastie, "The Common Knowledge Effect: Information Sharing and Group Judgment," *Journal of Personality and Social Psychology* 65, no. 5 (1993): 959–774.

31. C. Christensen et al., "Decision Making of Clinical Teams: Communication Patterns and Diagnostic Error," *Medical Decision Making* 20 (2000): 45–50.

32. P.B. Paulus and H.C. Yang, "Idea Generation in Groups: A Basis for Creativity in Organizations," *Organizational Behavior and Human Decision Processes* 82 (2000): 76–87, doi: 10.1006/obhd.2000.2888.

33. E. Salas et al., "The Science of Training and Development in Organizations: What Matters in Practice," *Psychological Science in the Public Interest* 13, no. 2 (2012): 74–101.

34. Burt, *Brokerage and Closure*.

35. "7 Truths Behind the 'Real' Work-Life Balance," *Employee Benefit News*, September 2, 2015 http://www.benefitnews.com/slideshow/7-truths -behind-the-real-work-life-balance.

36. M.T. Hansen and M.R. Haas, "Competing for Attention in Knowledge Markets: Electronic Document Dissemination in a Management Consulting Company," *Administrative Science Quarterly* 46, no. 1 (2001): 1–28.

37. C. Camerer, "Individual Decision Making," in *Handbook of Experimental Economics*, ed. J. Kagel and A. Roth (Princeton, NJ: Princeton University Press, 1995); R. Zweck and C-C. Lee, "Bargaining and Search: An Experimental Study," *Group Decision and Negotiation* 8, no. 6 (1999): 463–487.

38. R. Krulwich, "How to Marry the Right Girl: A Mathematical Solution. *Krulwich Wonders*, NPR.org, May 15, 2014, http://www.npr .org/sections/krulwich/2014/05/15/312537965/how-to-marry-the-right- girl-a-mathematical-solution.

39. Ibid

40. A. Mani et al., "Poverty Impedes Cognitive Function," *Science* 341, no. 6149 (2013): 976–980; and S. Mullainathan and E. Shafir, *Scarcity*: Why Having Too Little Means So Much (New York: Times Books, 2013).

41. B. Sullivan and H. Thompson, "Brain, Interrupted," *New York Times*, May 3, 2013, http://www.nytimes.com/2013/05/05/opinion/ sunday/a-focus-on-distraction.html.

42. C. Hooten, "Our Attention Span Is Now Less Than That of a Goldfish, Microsoft Study Finds," *Independent*, May 13, 2015, http:// www.independent.co.uk/news/science/our-attention-span-is-now-less-than- that-of-a-goldfish-microsoft-study-finds-10247553.html.

43. P.A. Mueller and D.M. Oppenheimer, "The Pen Is Mightier Than the Keyboard: Advantages of Longhand over Keyboard Notetaking," *Psychological Science* 25 (2014): 1159–1168.

44. J. Sovern, "Law Student Laptop Use During Class for Non-Class Purposes: Temptation v. Incentives," *University of Louisville Law Review* 51 (2013): 483–534. For a further discussion of these studies, see C. May, "A Learning Secret: Don't Take Notes with a Laptop," *Scientific American*, June 3, 2014, http://www.scientificamerican.com/ article/a-learning-secret-don-t-take-notes-with-a-laptop.

45. M. Csikszentmihalyi, *Flow: The Psychology of Optimal Experience* (New York: Harper and Row, 1990).

Chapter 6

1. "The Original Dream Team," *NBA Encyclopedia*, http://www.nba.com/history/dreamT_moments.html.

2. J. Kimble, "Ten Years Later, Revisiting Team USA's Flop in the 2004 Olympics," *Triangle Offence*, August 10, 2014, http://triangleoffense.com/features/ten-years-later-revisiting-team-usas-flop-in-the-2004-olympics/.

3. R. Lowenstein, *When Genius Failed: The Rise and Fall of Long-Term Capital Management* (New York: Random House, 2000).

4. K. Lewin, R. Lippit, and R.K. White, "Patterns of Aggressive Behavior in Experimentally Created Social Climates," *Journal of Social Psychology* 10 (1939): 271–301.

5. D. Johnson, "How Much Do Useless Meetings Cost?" *CBS Money Watch*, February 16, 2012, http://www.cbsnews.com/news/how-much-do-useless-meetings-cost/.

6. M.T. Hansen, "The Search-Transfer Problem: The Role of Weak Ties in Sharing Knowledge Across Organization Subunits," *Administrative Science Quarterly* 44, no. 1 (1999): 82–111. See also Morten Hansen's book on this subject, *Collaboration: How Leaders Avoid the Traps, Build Common Ground, and Reap Big Results* (Boston, MA: Harvard Business Review Press, 2009), and Henrik Bresman and Deborah Ancona's book *X Teams: How to Build Teams That Lead, Innovate, and Succeed* (Boston, MA: Harvard Business Review Press, 2007).

7. B.J. Robertson, *Holacracy: The New Management System for a Rapidly Changing World* (New York: Henry Holt, 2015).

8. B. Snyder, "Holacracy and 3 of the most unusual management practices around," *Forbes*, June 2, 2015, http://fortune.com/2015/06/02/management-holacracy/.

9. "Micromanaging in the Workplace," Accountemps, press release, http://accountemps.rhi.mediaroom.com/file.php/1597/Accountemps_Micromanaging_Infographic.jpg?utm_campaign=Press_Release&utm_medium=Link&utm_source=Press_Release.

10. J.C. Magee and A.D. Galinsky, "Social Hierarchy: The Self-Reinforcing Nature of Power and Status," *Academy of Management Annals* 2 (2008): 351–398.

11. J.R. Hackman and R. Wageman, "A Theory of Team Coaching," *Academy of Management Review* 30, no. 2 (2005): 269–287.

12. F. Laloux, *Reinventing Organizations* (Brussels, Belgium: Nelson Parker, 2014).

13. I.D. Steiner, *Group Processes and Productivity* (Waltham, MA: Academic Press, Inc., 1972).

14. M. Ringelmann, "Appareils de cultur mécanique avec treuils et cables (résultats d'essais)" (Mechanical tilling equipment with winches and cables [results of tests]), *Annales de l'Institut National Agronomique*,

2e serie—tome XII (1913): 299–343; M. Ringelmann, "Recherches sur les moteurs animés: Travail de l'homme (Research on animate sources of power: The work of man), *Annales de l'Institut National Agronomique*, 2e serie—tome XII (1913): 1– 40.

15. M. Diehl and W. Stroebe, "Productivity Loss in Brainstorming Groups: Toward a Solution of a Riddle," *Journal of Personality and Social Psychology* 53, no. 3 (1987): 497–509; F.M. Jablin, "Cultivating Imagination: Factors That Enhance and Inhibit Creativity in Brainstorming Groups," *Human Communication Research* 7, no. 3 (1981): 245–258; B. Mullen, C. Johnson, and E. Salas, "Productivity Loss in Brainstorming Groups: A Meta-Analytic Integration," *Basic and Applied Social Psychology* 12 (1991): 3–23; P.B. Paulus and M.T. Dzindolet, "Social Influence Processes in Group Brainstorming," *Journal of Personality and Social Psychology* 64 (1993): 575–586; P.B. Paulus, T.S. Larey, and A.H. Ortega, "Performance and Perceptions of Brainstormers in an Organizational Setting," *Basic and Applied Social Psychology* 17 (1995): 249–265; D.W. Taylor, P.C. Berry, and C.H. Block, "Does Group Participation When Using Brainstorming Facilitate or Inhibit Creative Thinking?" *Administrative Science Quarterly* 3 (1958): 23–47.

16. L. Thompson, *Creative Conspiracy* (Cambridge, MA: Harvard Business Review Press, 2013).

17. C.J. Nemeth and B. Nemeth-Brown, "Better Than Individuals? The Potential Benefits of Dissent and Diversity for Group Creativity," in *Group Creativity: Innovation through Collaboration*, ed. P. Paulus and B. Nijstad (Oxford: Oxford University Press, 2003), 63–84.

18. I.L. Janis, *Victims of Groupthink: A Psychological Study of Foreign Policy Decisions and Fiascoes* (Boston: Houghton Mifflin Company, 1972).

19. P.B. Paulus and H.C. Yang, "Idea Generation in Groups: A Basis for Creativity in Organizations," *Organizational Behavior and Human Decision Processes* 82 (2000): 76–87, doi: 10.1006/obhd.2000.2888.

20. E.F. Rietzschel, B. Nijstad, and W. Stroebe, "Productivity Is Not Enough: A Comparison of Interactive and Nominal Brainstorming Groups on Idea Generation and Selection," *Journal of Experimental Social Psychology* 44 (2006): 244–251.

21. M. Diehl and W. Stroebe, "Productivity Loss in Idea-Generating Groups: Tracking Down the Blocking Effect," *Interpersonal Relations and Group Processes* 61, no. 3 (1991): 392–403.

22. J. Surowiecki, *The Wisdom of Crowds* (New York, Doubleday, 2004).

23. N. Zeliadt, "Gaming the System: Video Gamers Help Researchers Untangle Protein Folding Problem," *Scientific American*, August 4, 2010, http://www.scientificamerican.com/article/gaming-the-system-video-gamers-help-researchers-untangle-protein-folding-problem/.

24. On those puzzles that the humans did better on, the scientists observed that the solvers could quickly see what was wrong, and then

solve it. What tripped up the computer was that the solution required solvers to restructure the problem in a way that would cause them to lose points initially; see Steiner, *Group Processes and Productivity.*

25. T. McCaffrey, "Why You Should Stop Brainstorming," *Harvard Business Review*, March 24, 2014, https://hbr.org/2014/03/why-you-should-stop-brainstorming/.

26. T. DeMarco and T. Lister, "Programmer Performance and the Effects of the Workplace," in *ICSE '85 Proceedings of the 8th International Conference on Software Engineering* (Los Alamitos, CA: IEEE Computer Society Press Los Alamitos, 1985): 268–272.

27. S. Cain, *Quiet: The Power of Introverts in a World That Can't Stop Talking* (New York: Crown Publishers, 2012).

28. R. Zajoncs, "Social Facilitation," *Science* 149, no. 3681 (1965): 269–274.

29. A. Pentland, "The New Science of Great Teams," *Harvard Business Review* (April 2012).

30. L. Thompson and T. Cohen, "Metacognitions in Teams and Organizations," in *Social Metacognitions*, ed. P. Brinol and K.G. DeMarree (New York: Psychology Press, 2012), 283–302.

31. A.W. Woolley et al., "Bringing in the Experts: How Team Composition and Collaborative Planning Jointly Shape Analytic Effectiveness," *Small Group Research* 39 (2008), 352–371.

32. J.M. Levine and R.L. Moreland, "Group Socialization: Theory and Research," *European Review of Social Psychology* 5, no. 1 (1994): 305–336.

33. M.A. West, "Innovation in Top Management Teams," *Journal of Applied Psychology* 81 (1996): 680–693; M.A. West, "Reflexivity, Revolution and Innovation in Work Teams," in *Product Development Teams: Advances in Interdisciplinary Studies of Work Teams*, ed. M. Beyerlein (Riverside, CA: JAI Press, 2000), 1–30.

34. D.W. Liang, R. Moreland, and L. Argote, "Group versus Individual Training and Group Performance: The Mediating Role of Transactive Memory," *Personality and Social Psychology Bulletin* 21 (1995): 384–393.

35. P.S. Goodman and S. Shah, "Familiarity and Work Group Outcomes," in *Group Processes and Productivity* (Newbury Park, CA: Sage, 1992).

36. J.R. Hackman, "Teams, Leaders, and Organizations: New Directions for Crew-Oriented Flight Training," in *Cockpit Resource Management*, ed. E.L. Wiener, B.G. Kanki, and R.L. Helmreich (San Diego, CA: Academic, 1993), 47–69.

37. I.G. Meister, T. Krings, B.B. Boroojerdi, M. Müller, R. Töpper, and A. Thron, "Playing piano in the mind—an fMRI study on music imagery and performance in pianists." *Cognitive Brain Research* 19, no. 3 (2004): 219–228. See also ed.ted.com/lessons/how-playing-an-instrument-benefits-your-brain-anita-collins.

38. R.L. Moreland and J.G. McMinn, "Group Reflexivity and Performance." in *Advances in Group Processes*, vol. 27, ed. S.R. Thye and E. Lawler (Bingley, UK: Emerald Press, 2010), 63–95.

39. D.W. Liang, R. Moreland, and L. Argote, "Group versus Individual Training and Group Performance," *Personality and Social Psychology Bulletin* 21, no. 4 (1995): 384–393.

40. D.C. Lau and J.K. Murnighan, "Interactions within Groups and Subgroups: The Effects of Demographic Faultlines," *Academy of Management Journal* 48, no. 4 (2005): 645–659.

41. J.M. Gottman, J. Coan, S. Carrere, and C. Swanson, "Predicting Marital Happiness and Stability from Newlywed Interactions," *Journal of Marriage and the Family* 60, no. 1 (1998): 5–22.

42. T. Menon and K. Phillips, "Getting Even or Being at Odds? Cohesion in Even- and Odd-Sized Groups," *Organization Science* 22, no. 3 (2011): 738–753.

43. A.C. Bluedorn and R.B. Denhardt, "Time and Organizations," *Journal of Management* 14, no. 2 (1988): 299–320.

44. J.E. McGrath, J.R. Kelly, and D.E. Machatka, "The Social Psychology of Time: Entrainment of Behavior in Social and Organizational Settings," *Applied Social Psychology Annual* 5 (1984): 21–44.

45. C. Gersick, "Marking Time: Predictable Transitions in Task Groups," *Academy of Management Journal* 32, no. 2 (1989): 274–309.

46. "Building a Better Cubicle," *CBS News*, January 31, 2002, http://www.cbsnews.com/news/building-a-better-cubicle/.

Chapter 7

1. Mahatma Gandhi, as quoted at: http://www.india.com/top-n/mahatma-gandhi-jayanti-top-15-memorable-and-inspiring-quotes-160998/.

Index

Note: page numbers followed by *f* refer to figures; page numbers followed by *t* refer to tables.

Agreement Trap
  avoidance of conflict and, 101–102
  avoidance of signals and, 93–94
  avoidance of voicing opinions
    and, 94, 95–96
  in close relationships, 104–107
  conclusion, 118
  described, 22–24
  diversity and, 102–104
  escaping (*see* escaping
    Agreement Trap)
  feedback presentation and
    (*see* feedback)
  fragile ego double standard,
    99–100
  fragile ego illusion, 97–99
  never events and, 91–92
  people's belief that others are
    intimated by them, 99–100
  psychological contracts between
    colleagues, 94–96
  self-censoring and, 92, 94
  signal distortion and, 107
  underlying motivation for, 95
Airbus, 11, 12
allotted time effect, 173–174
Apfelbaum, Evan, 103

background checks, 52
background signals awareness
  conflicts due to different cultures,
    53–54
  creation of blind spots and, 48–50

described, 36
fundamental attribution error
  and, 51–52
impact of individuals' behavior
  on situations, 53
managerial implications of, 50–51
tendency to miss signals, 48–49
Bazerman, Max, 79
Blount, Sally, 65
Bowling Alone (Putnam), 125
brainstorming
  brainswarming and, 158–159
  brainwriting and, 155–156
  ground rules of, 154–155
  record of effectiveness, 154
  value in criticism of ideas, 155
  verbal idea generation, 159–160
  wisdom of crowds and, 157–158
brainswarming, 158–159
brainwriting, 136, 155–156
Burt, Ron, 125
Butler, Paul, 129

*Cathedral and the Bazaar,
  The* (Raymond), 157
cave and commons, 161–163
Chakravarti, Arjun, 130
chaotic noise
  activating trade-off thinking, 143
  clarifying purpose of data and, 142
  costs in undersearching and
    oversearching, 140–142
  described, 122–123

chaotic noise (*continued*)
  flow and, 144–145
  personal signal-to-noise ratio
    and, 137–139
  screening out distractions, 143–145
  standards of testable hypotheses
    and, 142
  zerotasking and, 144
Chiu, Chi-Yue, 49, 53
Choi, Hoon Seok, 67
Cialdini, Robert, 115
common information effect, 135
Communication Trap
  bonding versus bridging ties, 125
  chaotic noise and, 122–123
  common information effect,
    135–136
  conclusion, 145–146
  described, 24–25, 120
  echo chambers and, 126
  escaping (*see* escaping
    Communication Trap)
  finding signal amid noise, 120
  managers' time investment in
    e-mails, 121, 138
  pros and cons of silos, 125–127
  quantity of communications,
    24–25
  redundant noise and, 122
  signal-detection theory and, 120
  sociograms, 123–125
  solution to, 121–122
  structural holes in networks,
    125–126
confirmation bias, 42–43, 48
conflict
  allotted time effect, 173–174
  amount spent per week dealing
    with, 12–13
  costs of personnel conflicts, 1–3,
    9, 10f, 12–13, 29–30
  due to different cultures, 53–54
  escaping Agreement Trap using,
    116–117, 118

group-level patterns, 171–173
  impasses caused by avoiding,
    101–102
  inevitability of, with superstars,
    168–169
  moving from conflict to cohesion,
    171–174
  people's tendency to avoid, 23,
    94, 95, 105
  rethinking brainstorming, 155
  symptoms of unproductive
    conflict, 169–171
culture
  Agreement Trap and, 93–94
  cave and commons and, 160–161
  comfort level for speaking up
    and, 114
  communication norms and, 121,
    130, 138
  differences in perspectives
    between, 49, 53

Daily Waste Score, 9, 10f, 29–31, 40
Dawes, Robyn, 46, 47
Dembélé, Moctar, 54, 55
diversity and Agreement Trap,
  102–104
Duncker, Karl, 56
Dunwell, Stephen, 87–88

Electronic Arts, 117
e-mails
  managers' time investment in,
    121, 138
  relationship of frequency to
    physical proximity, 25, 129–130
  screening out distractions from,
    143–145
  Type II costs of, 138
escaping Agreement Trap
  by how you deliver negative
    message, 115–116

using conflict, 116–117
using negotiation, 108–112
escaping Communication Trap
    activating trade-off thinking, 143
    brainwriting, 136
    breaking out of geographic
        habits, 129–130
    bringing diversity to your people,
        133–134
    changing conversation, 134–137
    changing your footpath at work,
        127–128
    clarifying purpose of data, 142
    costs in undersearching and
        oversearching, 140–142
    disciplining data search, 139–143
    emergent interactions' yielding of
        novel signals, 128
    encouraging bridging ties, 131
    flow and, 144–145
    leveraging underutilized common
        spaces, 132
    personal signal-to-noise ratio and,
        137–139
    screening out distractions,
        143–145
    standards of testable hypotheses
        and, 142
    using geography to overcome
        similarity, 130–133
    zerotasking and, 144
escaping Expertise Trap
    overview, 36–37
    pattern recognition and testing
        (see pattern detection and
        checking)
    problem finding before problem
        solving (see problem finding)
    seeing figure and ground (see
        background signals awareness)
escaping Macromanagement Trap
    allotted time effect, 173–174
    behaviors of groups that coalesce,
        163–164
developing common language,
    164–166
group-level patterns, 171–173
inevitability of conflict with
    superstars, 168–169
mental models use, 166–168
metacognition and, 164–165
perceptions about how decisions
    are made and, 165–166
symptoms of unproductive
    conflict, 169–171
escaping Winner's Trap
    anti free-riders' strategy, 81–83
    bringing in fresh eyes, 86–87
    eliminating financial incentives,
        77–79
    encouraging people to evaluate
        own strengths, 73–74
    giving dead projects funeral, 85,
        87–89
    problems with incentive
        packages, 76
    publicity as source of social
        influence, 82
    relational rewards, 76–77
    resources that can motivate
        people, 75–76
    rewarding accuracy, 87
Etsy, 88
Expertise Trap
    benefits of expertise, 34
    conclusion, 61
    consequences of failure to react to
        signals, 35–36
    described, 19–21
    escaping (see escaping
        Expertise Trap)
    example of failure of expertise,
        33–34
    satisficing and, 34

Facebook, 129–130
failure trap, 16

Faso Soap, 55
feedback
    controlling "why" in, 113–114
    interference effect from, 77
    problem of weak and distorted,
        101–102
    recipients' defensiveness and, 113
    sending clear signal, 114–116
    soft, 97
    using negative, then positive
        message approach, 115–116
flow, 144–145
Foldit, 158
"four horsemen of the apocalypse,"
    169–171
fragile ego illusion, 97–100
free riders, 81–83
Fresh Choice, 66
Fu, Jeanne, 49
fundamental attribution error,
    51–52

Galinsky, Adam, 68, 109
General Motors, 93, 95
groups. See teams

holacracy at Zappos, 151
Hong, Ying-Yi, 49, 53
horizontal trail-off, 160
human intuition, 47

illusion of progress, 17
incentives
    financial, 74, 78
    problems with packages, 71–72
    relational rewards, 76–77
    resources that can motivate
        people, 75–76
    results of eliminating financial,
        77–78
internal rivals, 22, 65, 67, 68, 73, 74

interviews and hiring
    confirmation bias during, 42–43
    designing to avoid biases, 44–45
    estimated costs of bad hires, 40
    pattern-fixation trap example,
        39–41
    using data from past hiring
        experiences, 45–48

Kerr, Steve, 70
Koch, Bradley, 116
Koch, Pamela, 116
Kray, Laura, 109

Laloux, Frederic, 152
Linus's law, 158
Loewenstein, George, 79
Long-Term Capital Management, 148

Macromanagement Trap
    brainstorming and, 154–156
    brainswarming and, 158–159
    brainwriting and, 155–156
    cave and commons and, 160–163
    conclusion, 174–175
    costs of hands-off management, 149
    described, 26–27
    escaping (see escaping
        Macromanagement Trap)
    key predictor of team's success,
        153–154
    managerial strengths as liabilities,
        150–151
    multiply-by-zero fallacy, 150
    process losses in groups, 153
    results when talented people can't
        work together, 147–149
    value equation for groups, 152
    value in hierarchies, 152
    verbal idea generation, 159–160
    wisdom of crowds, 157–158

malaria, 54–55
Mayer, Marissa, 160
McKinsey Global Institute, 121
Meggyesy, Dave, 71
Menon, Tanya, 37, 49, 53, 65, 66, 67, 68, 70, 82, 116, 130, 172
Meriwether, John, 148
Messick, David, 79
metacognition, 164–165
Moreno, Jacob, 124
Morris, Michael, 53
multiply-by-zero fallacy, 150
myside bias, 42

National Football League (NFL), 71–72
negotiation
    being strategic, 110–112
    categories of, 108
    challenging own stereotype, 109–110
    leveraging "nice" stereotype, 110
    problem with being "nice," 109
network activators, 135
network choking, 135
never events, 91–92
Nonaka, Ikujiro, 86
Nyondiko, Gérard, 54, 55

Occam's razor, 142
Osborn, Alex, 154
overfitting, 38
Owens, Terrell, 71

Parkinson's Law, 173–174
pattern detection and checking
    acceptance of untested patterns, 41
    described, 36
    estimated costs of bad hires, 40
    pattern-fixation trap example, 39–41

patterns' usefulness for organizing noise, 37–39
separating signal from noise (see signal separation)
statistical errors in seeing patterns, 38
top-down perception and, 39
Pentland, Sandy, 131, 163
people problems
    action without traction and, 4, 13–14
    amount spent per week dealing with conflict, 12–13
    associating new problems with old solutions and, 17
    challenge in stopping wicked problems, 17–18
    changing course too quickly and, 15–16
    characteristics of wicked problems, 6–8
    conclusion, 28–29, 191
    consequences of having wrong mental model, 15
    cost of personnel impasses, 1–3
    Daily Waste Score, 9, 10f, 29–31
    dollar cost estimates of wasted company time, 4
    fixating on substitute problems and, 15–16
    hidden waste of, 8–9
    key insights about, 5
    new team leader's dilemma (see Sandeep's journey)
    problem-solving approaches being used, 4
    reasons for misdirected action, 14
    spending traps surrounding (see spending traps)
    Type I and II waste, 11–13
Pfeffer, Jeffrey, 41, 66, 70
Phillips, Kathy, 116, 172
Platt, Lew, 65
Porter, Jay, 77

pre-utilization bias, 54–56
problem finding
  asking new set of questions,
    56–58
  being stuck in mental models and
    patterns, 54
  described, 37
  guiding questions, 60
  illustrating different points of
    view and, 58–59
  overcoming pre-utilization bias,
    54–56
  presenting resources to people in
    new way, 56
protective mother figure, 110
psychological contracts, 82, 94–96
Putnam, Robert, 125

Raymond, Eric, 157
redundant noise, 122
Rhode Island Hospital, 91–92
Riccitiello, John, 117

Sandeep's journey
  assessing options, 185–188
  basic problem with team, 184
  breaking down silos, 188–189
  characteristics of people problem,
    7–8
  costs of personnel conflicts, 1–3
  creeping self-interest and, 80
  dominance of competition over
    cooperation, 69–70
  illustrating different points of
    view and, 58–59
  keeping momentum going,
    189–190
  odd-sized group effect, 172–173
  problem finding, 56–58, 184–185
satisficing, 34
Schneier, Bruce, 16
secretary problem, 140–141

self-censoring, 92, 94
Sentis, Keith, 79
Shea, Catherine, 82
Sheldon, Oliver, 68
Shenkar, Oded, 116
signal-detection theory, 120
signal separation
  analyzing data from past
    experiences, 45–48
  challenging pattern and, 41–43
  confirmation bias, 42–44
  disconfirmation tests, 43, 48
signals versus noise in problem
    solving
  allowing noise to drown out signals
    (see Macromanagement Trap)
  associating new problems with
    old solutions and, 17
  challenge in stopping wicked
    problems, 17–18
  changing course too quickly and,
    15–16
  described, 13–14
  failure to translate signals clearly
    (see Agreement Trap)
  fixating on substitute problems
    and, 16–17
  fixation on faulty signals
    (see Expertise Trap)
  having wrong mental model and, 15
  ignoring signals (see Winner's Trap)
  missing signals
    (see Communication Trap)
  price of action without traction, 4
silo mentality
  breaking down in team, 188–189
  Communication Trap and, 122,
    125–127, 128, 131
  Winner's Trap and, 69
Sim, Jessica, 49
Simon, Herbert, 34
Smith, Ned, 135
smoker network, 127
sociograms, 123–124

spending traps, 5
  Agreement Trap, 22–24
  commonality of, 18
  Communication Trap, 24–25
  engaging team to escape, 182–183
  Expertise Trap, 19–21
  identifying where resources are
    wasted, 178–179
  Macromanagement Trap, 26–27
  root cause of, 177–178
  tackling inertia and, 181–182
  Winner's Trap, 21–22
  See also individual traps
spend-value matrix, 186–187
sprint reviews, 86–87
standardized protocols for
    interviews, 44–45
Steinem, Gloria, 111
Steiner, Ivan, 152
strategic negotiation, 111–112
Stretch computer (IBM), 87–88
subordinates, 93, 94, 97, 101–102
Sutton, Robert, 41
SWANS (strong women achievers,
    no spouse), 98

Takeuchi, Hirotaka, 86
teams
  allotted time effect, 173–174
  asking new questions, 56–58
  behaviors of groups that coalesce,
    163–164
  breaking down silo mentality in,
    188–189
  communication traps, 125
  costs of hands-off management, 149
  creating conditions for groups to
    coalesce, 164–168
  developing common language
    and, 164–166
  disconfirmation test for, 47–48
  fixing ones with problems, 46–48,
    56–60

group-level patterns, 171–173
guiding questions, 60
illustrate different points of view
    and, 58–59
inevitability of conflict with
    superstars, 168–169
key predictor of team's success,
    153–154
mental models use, 166–168
metacognition and, 164–165
moving from conflict to cohesion,
    169–174
multiply-by-zero fallacy, 150
perceptions about how decisions
    are made and, 165–166
process losses in groups, 153
results when talented people can't
    work together, 147–149
summary table, 180t
symptoms of unproductive
    conflict, 169–171
using data to maximize
    productivity potential, 46–47
value equation for groups, 152
Team USA, 147–148, 163
Thompson, Leigh, 65, 67, 79, 109,
    111, 129, 133, 164
tipping, 77
top-down perception, 39
Type I and II waste, 11–13

US Senate sociogram, 124

value equation for groups, 152
verbal idea generation, 159–162
vertical takeoff, 159–160
Volkswagen, 93, 95

Wang, Cindy, 37
Watson, Thomas, Jr., 87, 88
Whitson, Jennifer, 37

Williams, Serena, 66
Winner's Trap
  bias toward outsider
    information, 68
  companies' tendency to reward
    external learning, 70
  conclusion, 89–90
  cooperation among ants and,
    84–85
  creeping self-interest and, 79–80
  described, 21–22
  difficulty in relinquishing goal
    and, 85
  dilemma of rewarding A when
    hoping for B, 70–72
  dominance of competition over
    cooperation, 68–69
  financial exchanges' impact on
    social relationships, 76
  financial incentives and, 74,
    76–78
  interference effect from
    feedback, 77
  irony in trying to win in
    traffic, 64
  managers' shutting out of talented
    insiders, 66–67, 68
  merit of idea versus messenger, 65
  mixed messages about value, 72
  organizational traffic jams
    described, 64–65

overcommitting to ideas not
    working and, 83–84
  path to personal improvement
    and, 65–66
  people's difficulty in relinquishing
    goals, 85
  problems with incentive packages,
    71–72
  question of managers' disinterest
    in insiders' ideas, 68
  strategies for escaping
    (see escaping Winner's Trap)
  temptation to ignore or denigrate
    rivals, 66–67, 73
  waste resulting from ignoring
    rival's ideas, 65
Winship, Christopher, 130
wisdom of crowds, 157–158
women
  Agreement Trap from being
    "nice," 109
  leveraging "nice" stereotype, 110
  protective mother figure, 110
  SWANS image and, 98
Wooley, Anita, 164
wrong-site surgeries, 91–92

Zappos, 151
zerotasking, 144
Zoopa, 66

About the Authors

Tanya Menon is an associate professor at Fisher College of Business at the Ohio State University. Her research on leadership, collaboration, and global management has been cited in various media outlets including the *Wall Street Journal*, *Financial Times*, *Boston Globe*, The Economist Intelligence Unit, *Times of London*, *The Guardian* (UK), and the *Times of India*. Her latest research considers how people think about their networks and capture their value. She is currently an associate editor at the journal *Management Science*.

Menon is also a passionate teacher. She has won multiple teaching awards and, during her ten years as a professor at the University of Chicago Booth School of Business, her courses filled to capacity nearly every quarter. These courses combined theory with practical consulting projects in local nonprofits. She also co-taught a popular leadership course with Chicago-area chief executive officer Lee Hillman. She has done keynotes and executive programs all over the world. Her fine-grained operational consulting at a *Fortune* 500 company for over five years led to measurable gains as it achieved award-winning customer service outcomes.

Menon's undergraduate thesis on urban poverty, under the direction of Professor Chris Winship, was awarded a Hoopes Prize as one of Harvard University's top theses. She received her PhD from Stanford Graduate School of Business. Before entering graduate school, Menon was a research assistant at

INCAE Business School in Costa Rica and an intern in Morgan Stanley's London office.

For more information about Tanya Menon, please see: menon.socialpsychology.org.

Leigh Thompson is an internationally recognized scholar on negotiation, group decision making, team creativity, teamwork, and collaboration. Thompson is the J. Jay Gerber Distinguished Professor of Dispute Resolution & Organizations at the Kellogg School of Management at Northwestern University. She is the author of eleven books, including: *Creative Conspiracy: The New Rules of Breakthrough Collaboration*; *Making the Team: A Guide for Managers*; *The Mind and Heart of the Negotiator*; and *The Truth About Negotiations*.

Thompson is the director of Kellogg's Leading High Impact Teams executive program, Negotiation Strategies executive program, and Constructive Collaboration executive program. Thompson does research and teaching around the globe. Among her books, *The Truth About Negotiations* is a best-seller and has been translated into seven languages; *The Mind and Heart of the Negotiator* has been translated into four languages; and *Making the Team* has been translated into two languages.

Thompson created the popular High Performance Collaboration MOOC and the online video teaching series Negotiation 101 and Teamwork 101 for managers and executives. In addition, she has created the three-minute animated videos *Is Your Team Slacking?*, *Managing Virtual Teams*, *High-Performance Negotiation Skills for Women*, and *How Brainstorming Can Neutralize the Loudmouths*.

Leigh's work on team creativity has appeared in *Fast Company* and *BusinessWeek*. She serves on the editorial boards of several academic journals and is a member of the Academy of Management.

For more information about Leigh Thompson, visit her website: http://leighthompson.com/.